M000211908

FOREWORD BY RYAN LESTRANGE

kingdom mindset

A GUIDE TO LIVING A LIFE OF BREAKTHROUGH & MIRACLES

JOE JOE DAWSON

Copyright © 2018 by Joe Joe Dawson

All rights reserved. This book or any portion thereof may not be reproduced or used in any manner whatsoever without the express written permission of the publisher except for the use of brief quotations in a book review or scholarly journal.

First Printing: 2018

ISBN: 978-0-692-05949-4

ACKNOWLEDGEMENT

I want to thank my lady, Autumn Dawson and my daughter, Malachi Jewels Dawson for the title and subtitle of this book.

Special thanks to Ryan LeStrange for writing the foreword for this book. I also want to thank Jeff and Michelle McFarland and Elizabeth Fadare for helping me put this book together.

FOREWORD

T here is something about a breakthrough word, a breakthrough atmosphere and a breakthrough anointing! It will absolutely shift every area of your life. The reality is that the power of God can suddenly and dramatically break down every barrier to propel you forward. Right now, you may be facing areas of opposition and bondage. What you need is a sudden and miraculous breakthrough. You need the power of God to advance you.

I have always believed that one of the markers of an authentic apostolic anointing is liberty. God raises governing and building leaders to break people and places loose. He releases apostolic authority and anointing to bring divine liberty and freedom.

The Spirit of the Lord is upon me, because he hath anointed me to preach the gospel to the poor; he hath sent me to heal the brokenhearted, to preach deliverance to the captives, and recovering of sight to the blind, to set at liberty them that are bruised. Luke 4:18

In this passage Jesus announced five dimensions of the manifest anointing. I want to call your attention to the last dimension, setting at liberty them that are bruised. I believe these words speak about one of the divine attributes of the person of Holy Spirit but also they represent the apostolic anointing. Kingdom building cannot and will not happen without breakthrough. Cities will not be shaken without breakthrough. Nations will not be transformed without breakthrough. There is breakthrough for people and regions! The apostolic breaks down barriers and removes burdens to shift people into ordained plans.

Apostles and apostolic people are breakthrough people. They sing breakthrough songs. They preach breakthrough messages. They pray breakthrough prayers. They refuse to sit idly by in the dead courts of religion. They are up marching, advancing and leaping forward. They are power people and vision people!

The word Apostle means a *sent one*. Apostolic people don't just show up. They are divinely commissioned by God to manifest the breakthrough. They root out and tear down demonic systems and schemes. This is why the level of warfare around apostolic people can be very intense, but they are anointed to contend and persevere.

You are sent on an assignment. You may not feel it right now, but you have a powerful prophetic destiny. Heaven has ordained you for a beautiful purpose. In order for you to walk into your destiny, you may need a breakthrough. That is why you are picking up this book! These pages will inspire you and set you up for heaven's breakthrough plan for you.

Joe Joe Dawson is a dear friend, a passionate revivalist and a powerful front-line apostolic leader. He carries a prophetic sound that manifests the breakthrough everywhere he goes. He has heard from heaven by penning the words on these pages. As you read, you are going to be equipped and overcome by the prophetic anointing in this writing.

I declare the breakthrough of heaven over you in every area. I declare emotional breakthrough and financial breakthrough. I decree breakthrough in your family in Jesus' name. I say that every lying devil is exposed and every scheme brought down. I say that every plan and purpose of the Lord shall come to fruition in your life. I release the spirit of the breaker over you. You will not be held back any longer. You will be supernaturally propelled into heaven's plans and purposes for your life in Jesus' name!

Ryan LeStrange
Best Selling Author of Supernatural Access, Founder of iHubs,
RLM & TRIBE

KINGDOM MINDSET

CHAPTER 1
BREAKTHROUGH

Breakthrough! This word elicits great excitement in most Pentecostal and Charismatic circles. Many messages have been preached and songs written on the topic of breakthrough. Honestly, how many conferences or conventions have you been to that were titled "Breakthrough?" Many, am I correct? What is the main purpose for breakthrough? Is it so we will simply be free? Maybe we could even go deeper to the root of why we need breakthrough. To be in need of a breakthrough means that we are bound by something or have something blocking our progress toward our Heavenly assignment or in life in general. We like to believe that our breakthrough will be a sudden boom or bang at the altar of one of those powerful conference gatherings. I have personally had many breakthrough encounters at such altars. I have also had many breakthrough encounters in my private prayer times as well. There are numerous ways we can and will receive our breakthrough, but after we receive it, then what?

The word breakthrough means: "Sudden, dramatic, and important discovery or development." Let us go a step further in our thinking about this important subject. God strongly desires to bless us because He is wild about us, but He also wants us completely free to carry out the mission of His Kingdom. Whenever God grants an increase in our life, there is always a divine kingdom purpose attached. Many times we receive our miracles or breakthrough then go back to life as usual. God wants us to walk in complete freedom in this hour in order to effectively fulfill our Kingdom purpose on this earth.

Whenever we are in need of a breakthrough in life, we must remember that the attack or the warfare we are presently going through is only temporary. 1 Corinthians 10:13 states that, "No temptation has overtaken you except such as is common to man; but God is faithful, who will not allow you to be tempted beyond what you are able, but with the temptation will also make the way of escape, that you may be able to bear it." God will never let the trial, test, or tribulation completely overtake you. God is your way of escape! When we focus upon the Lord with all of our heart, he will give us the wisdom and revelation to get through any circumstance or situation. In the bible, the word heart is divided into two elements: the spirit and the soul. The soul is also divided into two parts: the mind and the emotions. When we fix our spirit, mind, and emotions upon the things of the Lord, His Holy Spirit promises to guide us and lead us into all truth and understanding in every situation (John 16:13; John 14:26).

If we could learn to embrace our warfare moments in the hard times, we would see that the Lord does His best work when we are in trouble. Psalm 46:1 tells us that "God is our refuge and strength; a very present help in times of trouble." We need to keep our daily walk with God strong through the reading of His word and through prayer and fasting. Whenever hard times come, we will know that He is the Good Shepherd and a safe place of refuge for us. As such, we can rest assured knowing that no strategic attack of the enemy will ever overtake us. Isaiah 54:17 "No weapon that is formed against thee shall prosper; and every tongue that shall rise against thee in judgment, thou shalt condemn. This is the heritage of the servants of the LORD, and their righteousness is of me, says the LORD." Our hope and trust are in the Lord alone.

The key to living a steadfast, victorious life in the good times and the bad is to keep our focus on the Lord and on what He is saying over our life. Proverbs 4:25-27 says, "Let your eyes look directly forward, and your gaze be straight before you. Ponder the path of your feet; then all your ways will be sure. Do not swerve to the right or to the left; turn your foot away from evil." We must keep our spirit very sensitive to the Holy Spirit. The Lord is always speaking to us and to our churches, cities, and regions. He is looking for people who will stand in the gap for Him to release breakthrough and open up entire regions toward the things of God. As we pray and contend for breakthrough, we must be wise in our warfare to ensure that we are always operating in the spirit of God. Do not fret and work yourself up so much waiting on your breakthrough that when it finally happens, you are too worn out to function effectively in it! When times of trouble hit, remember that God uses such seasons to stretch, prepare, and train you up as a good soldier. You do not get stronger in the good times. You only get stronger by enduring and persevering through times of adversity! Always keep in mind that the devil never goes to battle where there are no spoils. When you find your true identity in God and have come into the awareness of your God-given purpose and destiny, the enemy will launch his strongest and most vehement attacks. This is because he does not want the children of God to understand or walk in the full measure of the authority and power given to them by God.

As I was praying about a speaking engagement on breakthrough one day, the Lord gave me this paragraph: "Sometimes the breakthrough is simply the end of the process that God was using to take you toward a certain destination! You must learn to endure and allow the process to teach and grow you. Do not sit around and cry and complain or you will not learn what you desperately need to for your next level assignment. If you do not break, you will have your breakthrough! God will use the hard times to prepare you. These times will be full of pressure, but you will come out properly equipped for your next season. Take courage; your breakthrough is at hand!"

The enemy will always try to wear you out and tire you out with a steady stream of intense warfare whenever he senses you are getting close to breakthrough. You must always remember to not look at where you are, but rather at where you are going. Never focus on the area in which you need breakthrough, but choose instead to hone in on the promises God has made to you with clarity, dogged determination, and faith. Each obstacle is simply a hurdle put in your way to slow you down or distract you.

You need to make sure that you surround yourself with people of great faith. I would strongly advise you to remove all negative people from your sphere of influence. Negative and toxic people will always try to speak doubt into your life. If they ever managed to get a seed of doubt lodged in your soul, it will take longer for you to receive breakthrough because of the potency of those negative words that God never intended to be planted into your life. Just as God puts people around you to strengthen you, the enemy always puts people in your path to try to slow down the plans from heaven for your life.

You need to make sure that you have mentors—Apostles, Prophets, Pastors, and other mature, solid men and women of God—in your life who want you to succeed in all that God has for you. You need to make sure that you've got some people in your life who have been through hard situations, and have overcome test and trials that would have knocked most people out. These are people of great faith who stand strong when adversity is at the door. They are the ones who have learned to overcome and will teach and counsel you in how to do the same!

Hebrews 6:12 says, "We do not want you to become lazy, but to imitate those who through faith and patience inherit what has been promised." One of the main reasons the Lord will sometimes allow us to wait on His promises is to help us develop patience. This is a critical lesson that He needs us to learn. Many times we try to speed up the process, but God desires to teach us through the process. When I am in seasons of warfare, I have learned to cooperate with God so that I grow through the process and not just go through it. Every test and trial is a learning experience and will make you smarter and stronger for the days ahead.

We need to have faith, big faith! Believe 100% that God will come through for you because He will! That kind of faith attracts the favor of God and releases radical fulfillment of His promises!!! As we touched on before, Hebrews 6:12 talks about faith and patience. In faith, we have confidence in God's nature and can walk with patience and endurance through difficult circumstances because we know God will always come through in His timing for us. The words of Jesus in John 15:7 gives us added assurance of this. It says, "If you abide in Me, and My words abide in you, you will ask what you desire, and it shall be done for you." When you make it a daily practice to abide in God, you attract His favor, blessings, and increase. The Lord always wants us to have life-altering conversations and fellowship with Him. Like any good father, He always desires to draw us into His confidence and impart His wisdom, knowledge, understanding, and revelation to us.

John 15:4 says, "Remain in me, as I also remain in you. No branch can bear fruit by itself; it must remain in the vine. Neither can you bear fruit unless you remain in me." God is always looking for people who are determined to be productive for His Kingdom. He wants to raise up tenacious people who will fight through any adverse circumstance to complete the task He has set before them. Whenever we receive a prophetic word from the Lord it seems like the enemy attacks us from every angle and in every shape, form, and fashion. God is looking for people who will receive a true word from Him and hang on to that word for dear life. He wants people to live like their very life depends on this word, because it does. Always remember that He is the God of the great breakthrough in your life.

You see, friends, when you are on the cutting edge of what God is doing, you will always have a constant prophetic flow in your life. You have seen many people in business, worship, preaching etc. that are always on the very cutting edge of their industry or ministry. These people are the ones who are the forerunners running ahead with that prophetic flow. They are not afraid to push the envelope of what the Lord is currently saying. These types of people usually live lives full of warfare. The enemy constantly fights them because they are always on the edge of radical breakthrough in their lives. They are God's key players destined to release catastrophic destruction in the enemy's camp and significant breakthrough in the lives of many people and over many regions and nations. If you know you are one of these people, take courage. The Lord is with you. He is fighting for you and has never lost a battle! Be greatly encouraged by the fact that God desires to see you walk in breakthrough in every area of your life and fulfill your divinely-ordained destiny even more than you do!

Prophetic words are meant to bring confirmation not information. Many times people will ask a prophetic person to give them a word that will help direct their future. This is scary because a prophetic word is supposed to be confirmation of a word that you have already gotten from the Lord yourself. When we hear the voice of God for ourselves, we will be able to hang on to what He has spoken to us with much stronger faith when the hard times come. When we lean on a word that someone else gave us, when the hard times come, we may experience a stronger tendency to doubt its probability. When you receive a word from the Lord directly, the Holy Spirit gives you divine grace, strength, and stamina to hang on to that word until you see it fulfilled in your life.

Whenever you discover the purpose for which God created you, it will completely reshape your life and transform your very existence. Some people call it "finding your why." You begin to get divine revelation on life's most important questions, such as "Why am I here God?" "What is my purpose?" etc. When you begin to receive the answers to these questions, you will realize why the enemy has fought you so hard. This is why he is fights so relentlessly against your health, finances, emotional and mental well-being, relationships, focus, time, etc. The enemy is determined to do everything within his power to prevent you from functioning in your

Kingdom calling, because he understands that whenever someone receives true freedom from everything that has tried to blind and bind them, there is no stopping that person. When God has a son or daughter walking in complete freedom, they will do extreme damage to the enemy's camp and the enemy knows this.

CHAPTER 2
PATIENCE IN THE DELAY

We have to learn numerous lessons as God's children and one of every believer's favorites is the lesson of patience. This Christ-like virtue is actually an amazing tool if we can see the value in it. We need to realize that God does not waste anything or any amount of time. The reason we have to wait for breakthrough many times is because God is working things out in us. Always remember that God is working more things out behind-the-scenes in your life than you may realize. God is always up to something good and delights in setting you up to receive your breakthrough and every blessing on the other side of it.

When God gives us an amazing prophetic word, thought, or dream, we want it to be happen now. In reality, God gives us these prophetic insights to allow us time to get our heart (spirit, mind, and emotions) aligned with Him and His divine purpose for our life. We need to be fully prepared for what God has stored up for us. There is always a promise attached to the process that God is taking us through.

Isaiah 54:1 says, "Sing, O barren, you who have not borne! Break forth into singing, and cry aloud, you who have not labored with child! For more are the children of the desolate than the children of the married woman," says the Lord. "Enlarge the place of your tent, and let them stretch out the curtains of your dwellings; do not spare; lengthen your cords, and strengthen your stakes."

Barrenness means not having fruit or not able to produce. Just because you may have been barren in the past does not mean the same will be true of your future. One of our biggest problems is that we look into the natural realm too much and do not truly train our spiritual senses to discern the things of the supernatural realm enough. What about you? Do you believe what you see in the natural more than what you hear in the spirit? When the Holy Spirit speaks to us concerning any matter, that should settle it in our hearts (spirit, mind, and emotions). Never force the process nor the time frame because God is strategically at work preparing us and the promise for us. We should pray for God to strengthen us to endure and persevere faithfully just as much as we pray for the breakthrough to happen.

When God says you are going to have something, know that you are going to have whatever He says. Act like you believe it and begin to prepare for it by faith. If the Lord says you are going to have a child, get the nursery room ready and begin to stock up on baby items. Start preparing now! If God says He wants you to launch a side business, start on the paper work to get it set up right away. If God has said He is going to connect you with His choice of a kingdom spouse for your life, do your part by working on becoming as completely whole and healthy as possible so that you are prepared to transition smoothly into that season of blessing when it is time.

Partnering with God for your breakthrough means making concrete preparations for your blessing even before it arrives. This will help pave the way for a smooth transition to the reality of its manifestation. I always laugh and find it amusing in prayer meetings with zealous young people who say "God send me to the nations; I'm yours, Lord!" After praying, I gently ask them if they have a passport? 90% of the time, they say no. My friends, how can God do what you are believing Him for if you have not done your part to position yourself for it? Do not waste any more time! Get yourself into position now! By faith start moving toward the word of the Lord!

Four key words from Isaiah 54:2 are enlarge, stretch, lengthen, and strengthen. These words are action words. The Lord wants you to move by faith and prepare a place for His word to be manifested. God wants you to build a dwelling place for all His promises to come to pass. Where is your faith level on the promises you have from God? Are you building toward them being manifested or are you just sitting idle waiting? I have always loved the good, old Charismatic saying: "You've got to dance in advance!" That's right; praise God in advance!

Please understand that this passage means that when those who have long been barren finally begin to experience fruitfulness, they will have a higher rate to produce fruit faster than those who have been fruitful all along. This is because the supernatural rate of production is faster than that of the natural. What you will ultimately produce will be far greater than the ones you are looking at with fruit already. This will be the case for you, not just in quantity alone, but in the quality of your harvest as well. Take a look at the biblical account of Hannah in 1 Samuel chapters 1 and 2. Though she endured through a long and painful season of barrenness, when she finally received her answer from the Lord, she ended up giving birth to a mighty prophet.

The Bible makes no mention of any of Peninnah's children by name, but Hannah's son, Samuel, went on to play an incredibly significant role among the children of Israel at that pivotal time in the history of God's people. He was Hannah's long-awaited reward and her vindication for a prolonged season of barrenness. Therefore, take courage and purpose in your heart to find joy in the promise God has made to you even before the fulfillment manifests! Oftentimes, delayed answers come with greater increase. Delayed answers help to develop character and integrity. Anyone can celebrate after the answer comes, but God looks for the one who celebrates before the answer comes in the natural. When God speaks a promise to you, settle it in your heart that it will come to pass! Position yourself for the increase! Stretch your tent pegs and expand your capacity to receive in anticipation of the breakthrough!

CHAPTER 3
REST IN THE WARFARE

Whenever we are in desperate need of breakthrough, we usually are in a season of warfare. When under attack, sometimes we allow our emotions to get the best of us. Numerous times we overthink things and become very analytical. Oftentimes, we get fearful and anxious, and we can begin to feel insecure and nervous. What if I was to tell you that what we need to do most in these types of seasons is to relax. Yes, relax! Simple as that! The word of the lord unto those of you who are reading this right now is to cast your cares upon the Lord and relax!

Psalm 86:7 says, "In the day of my trouble, I will call upon You, for You will answer me." This verse brings so much comfort to many people. When you call upon God, He will always hear you. Even better, He will always answer you. How amazing is it to know that our Father will always hear our cry. Psalm 116:1 says, "I love the Lord, because He has heard my voice." In a world full of illegitimacy, it is so reassuring to know that our heavenly Father hears our cries. Psalms 17:6 says, "I have called upon You, for You will hear me, O God; Incline Your ear to me, and hear my speech." To know that our God hears every single word out of our mouth is so reassuring, and even better than that, He acts upon the words. He is faithful to release His miracle-working, explosive breakthrough power to act on our behalf.

God knows that we will go through hard situations and experience warfare moments in our lives in general. When we read scriptures where the Lord is asking us to call upon Him, it lets us know our heavenly Father is waiting for us to cry out to Him for breakthrough. In Psalm 50:15, the Lord tells us to "Call upon Me in the day of trouble." We have to realize that sometimes when we call upon the Lord, He does not always answer us right away because He is working out situations on our behalf. One day in prayer, the Lord spoke to me and said, "I'm doing more for you behind the scenes then you could ever imagine." So, when you pray, know that God hears and trust that He is moving in that situation. We may not see the hand of God moving in the natural but understand that, in the supernatural, it is moving like a whirlwind. Psalm 40:1 says, "I waited patiently for the Lord; and He inclined to me, and heard my cry."

I believe that Kingdom breakthrough is coming to many people's lives to bring about Kingdom increase. We are about to see numerous people experience radical breakthrough and rise up to answer the call that God has on their life. The reason I believe so many people have been in such great seasons of warfare is because their breakthrough is going to be at a level that we have never seen before. The harder we get pressed by the enemy, the harder we need to press into God. This makes us great ground for God to sow seeds of destiny into. If you plant decent seed into decent ground, you get a decent harvest. If you plant good seed into good ground, you get a good harvest. If you plant great seed into great ground, you get a great harvest. If you plant a God seed into someone who has allowed God to cultivate their heart, you get a God harvest! We are in the greatest days of harvest that we have ever known, and it is right before us. This is one of the reasons you have gone through what you have so that when you come out on the other side, you will be able to withstand any attack of the enemy.

Now let me help you learn how to relax while you are waiting on your breakthrough. Psalm 23:5 says, "You prepare a table before me in the presence of my enemies. You anoint my head with oil; my cup overflows." When the enemy has surrounded you, and is pressing you from every possible angle in every circumstance and situation of your life and you do not think you can handle anything else, this is when God most wants you to relax. You see, when you are in a warfare season and are going through a rough situation, you really do not want to eat or relax. Many people are too nervous and anxious in such seasons, but the Lord wants to prepare for you a table. Not a fast food meal in a sack; I'm talking about laying out for you a banquet table.

Now I don't know what your favorite meals and gourmet delicacies are, but my table has the juiciest, prime steak cooked medium-rare and a wide assortment of delicious sushi rolls. Then the Lord is going to have you sit down to enjoy this amazing meal and have fellowship with Him while He makes the enemy sit there and watch you enjoy this meal in total peace.

Oftentimes, the enemy will raise up critics to attack you in different areas, but they will not succeed I their assignment against your destiny, in Jesus' name! Instead, they will have to watch you walk in continuous success as God brings you through the breakthrough moments of your life and gives you incredible favor and increase. They will have to watch the Lord honor and elevate you and take you from glory to glory in every single area of your life!

This is why you need to never speak negatively of other people, because the Lord will cause you to witness their elevation and success. When God blesses you—and, yes, He is going to bless you—make sure you keep your heart right. Do not get arrogant or boastful, nor allow your heart to be lifted up in pride. Just sit down and enjoy the meal that the Lord has prepared for you and be very thankful for all He has brought you through. Then, the Scripture says that God is going to anoint your head. When you are anointed, the extreme power of God flows through you and touches everything that you do. When you are anointed, there is an added measure of increase and God's grace upon everything you do. Your enemies are going to have to watch God anoint your head with oil. Then, the Scripture tells us that God will cause your cup to overflow.

You see, in the past season, you did not feel anointed. You were not sitting at a table and your cup certainly was not overflowing. But things have changed and now your cup is overflowing. If, in the natural, there was a cup on a banquet table that was being poured into and was overflowing, everyone seated around the table would take note of it. In much the same way, you will have the pleasure of sitting down to enjoy an elegant meal and enjoy blessings galore in superabundance while all of your enemies are forced to watch. God Himself will anoint you with fresh oil and cause your cup to overflow at an extreme level. Your blessings are going to be so strong in the midst of your breakthrough that they are going to overtake you. You see, it is impossible for a child of God to be mad at any of their enemies when their cup runs over. In fact, the Lord will use you to show His love to those that did you wrong and talked badly about you. When you are anointed and your cup runs over, you will be full from the Lord's table. You will be full of forgiveness as well and will harbor ill will against no one. God desires His Kingdom children to walk in extreme increase and complete fullness in every area.

There is something that we all must understand. We like to pray "God hide me from my enemies," but that is not really how it works. Psalm 143:9 says, "Rescue me from my enemies, LORD, for I hide myself in you." You hide yourself from the enemy in God, but God doesn't hide you from the enemy; He just protects you. When your kids are little and grandparents come over to the house, the children leave your side and run straight up to the grandparents. The grandparents love to lean down or get on their knees and embrace the child. Now, although the child can no longer see the parents which they just ran from to fully embrace their grandparents, the parents can see the grandparents and vice versa. At

Roar Church Texarkana, I use my sweet daughter, Judah Macy Dawson, as an illustration of this. I had Judah come up from the front row and give me a hug. I could see the congregation and the congregation could see Judah, but Judah could see nothing but me. When we run to God, He fully embraces us. The enemy then says "We're in trouble now." I imagine he also says something like, "We better not touch this one." When we are in the full embrace of God and are abiding in Him, the enemy can by no means touch nor harm us.

Psalm 27:5-6 says, "For in the time of trouble He shall hide me in His pavilion; In the secret place of His tabernacle He shall hide me; He shall set me high upon a rock. And now my head shall be lifted up above my enemies all around me." You see, when we are hidden in God, the enemy might try to get near to surround us but neither he nor his demons can touch us because the Lord is our sure protection and covering. A pavilion is a structure that is completely covered overhead but has no walls around it. We take comfort in the sure promise of God's protection found in Psalm 91:1-2 which says, "He who dwells in the secret place of the Most High shall abide under the shadow of the Almighty." I will say of the Lord, "He is my refuge and my fortress; My God, in Him I will trust." We must always remember to run toward God in all situations and circumstances in life, especially when we are in the midst of intense seasons of warfare. Whenever we find ourselves in such seasons, it is because the enemy knows that we are on the verge of a mighty breakthrough that will help establish the Kingdom of God on the earth. The devil never goes to battle where there are no spoils. Always remember what a precious treasure you are to God. His Kingdom people are about to receive increase that is designed for Kingdom purposes! You get to steward the increase!

CHAPTER 4
MIRACLES

One of my favorite things about the ministry of Jesus Christ on earth is the miracles He performed. When Jesus taught, He spoke mostly of the Kingdom of God. Miracles would always happen before or after He taught. Jesus wanted people to know that when He spoke it was not just about His words alone but also the power that God the Father gave Him to move and operate in. He also taught the twelve disciples that they would have the power and authority to speak God's word, teach about His Kingdom, and walk in the authority that accompanied His dunamis power. Luke 10:19 says, "Behold, I give unto you power to tread on serpents and scorpions, and over all the power of the enemy: and nothing shall by any means hurt you."

I want every person reading this book to understand that you have authority from heaven to change the atmosphere that you are in. You have the authority and power to shift every geographical atmosphere you enter in. We have such a powerful authority given to us by God to lay hands on the sick and see them recover. We can declare over physical, spiritual, emotional, financial, mental, and marital situations and see them completely changed for the best. We have so much power available to us in Christ Jesus that we have not yet even tapped into. The Lord has placed so much authority and power in our grasp and many times we just let it slip away untapped. Someone else's miracle could be in your mouth, but sometimes we doubt ourselves and hesitate to even speak it. When we as God's children arise and realize who we are and—more importantly—whose we are, this truth will change our families, churches, businesses, ministries, cities, regions, friends, governments, and nations. Most times, we just need to realize and firmly believe that we can do everything the bible says we can do.

Matthew 8:2-3 says, "And behold, a leper came and worshiped him saying, 'Lord, if you are willing, you can make me clean.' Then Jesus put out his hand and touched him saying, 'I am willing; be cleansed.' And immediately his leprosy was cleansed." Whenever I read this passage, for some reason I always laugh. Could you imagine the response of Jesus? I imagine Him giving a small, short laugh with a heart full of love behind it. I can imagine Him saying, "Of course I love you and of course I am willing to heal you; why do you think I came! You see, Jesus came, for our salvation and healing and to demonstrate the Kingdom of God. Many people go to the Lord with an uncertain mindset, asking: "Lord, if You are willing, please move on my behalf." Thankfully, Jesus Christ took away all of our uncertainty in approaching Him by assuring us in Matthew 7:11 and Luke 11:13 that we have a good Father who delights in giving good things and doing wonders on behalf of His children.

We must understand some very important things when it comes to the miracles of God. The first one is how much He loves us; the second is that He does indeed want to perform miracles for us. In Mark 10:27, Jesus looked at them and said, "With man this is impossible, but not with God; all things are possible with God." We can never limit God to our human understanding and thinking. God desires to move on your behalf and manifest the Kingdom of God for you. I remember when I preached a weekend full of meetings, and about thirty minutes into the service on Sunday morning, the Lord spoke to me and said "Tell the people I am going to heal every single person that is here." In obedience, I boldly proclaimed the word that the Lord gave me and instructed the people to come up for healing.

The first gentleman was blind in one eye. My good friend, Jeff McFarland, prayed for him until he began to see out of both eyes. The second person had been deaf in one ear for many years. We prayed and she received complete restoration of her hearing in both ears. We prayed and prayed and when we were done, every person that we laid hands on and prayed for in that place was healed just as the Lord had said. We then got a report that there was a gentleman in a hospital in need of healing. We anointed an Appeal to Heaven flag and his family took it to the hospital and placed it on him. He was in a coma and had been diagnosed with a brain aneurysm. Before we left town, we received the testimony that he had awakened and sat up in his hospital bed. The next time I returned to that city, he was back on his job.

Luke 18:27 says, "Jesus replied, "What is impossible with man is possible with God." When we start to pray for supernatural miracles to happen in the lives of people, we have to get our mind off the natural realm because we can do nothing outside the miraculous, wonder-working power of Jesus Christ. In the natural, it may seem impossible, but all things are possible with God. When you ask God to step into any situation, He will turn every negative thing around and reverse it to a positive outcome. In Mark 9:23, Jesus says, "Everything is possible for the one who believes." Smith Wigglesworth once said, "Only believe!" God is looking for those of us in this hour who will boldly declare His word and allow Him to use us to demonstrate His miracle-working power!

I have made a practice, in my day-to-day life, of challenging people to believe God for miracles regardless of their circumstances. When someone tells me about their extremely difficult and impossible situation, I simply say, "Let's pray and declare right now and watch what God does." As a result, my wife, Autumn, and I have witnessed countless reports of miracles coming back the same day or a few days later in the impossible situations of people we have been blessed to pray for and stand in faith with. Together, we have seen numerous financial breakthroughs, physical healings, relationship mending, business turnarounds, creative ideas, ministry breakthroughs, and the list goes on and on. Jeremiah 32:27 says, "I am the Lord, the God of all mankind. Is anything too hard for me?" God is looking for people of faith to step up and step out and believe

Him for breakthrough and miracles to start happening in their day-to-day life.

Matthew 9:20-22 tells the story of the woman with the issue of blood. It says, "And suddenly, a woman who had a flow of blood for twelve years came from behind and touched the hem of His garment. For she said to herself, "If only I may touch His garment, I shall be made well." But Jesus turned around, and when He saw her He said, "Be of good cheer, daughter; your faith has made you well." And the woman was made well from that hour." To this day, many still refer to this lady as the woman who had the flow of blood, but Jesus simply referred to her as daughter. We have to quit looking at people and labeling them by their weakness, past failure, infirmity, or situation. Every person is either a son or daughter of God. The Lord is looking for people who are willing to disregard labels and stigma and partner with Him to bring healing, deliverance, and breakthrough to His children. God is always looking and longing for willing vessels to get out of their comfort zone. He wants to see all of His people walk in the full measure of authority He has given to greatly demonstrate His mighty power.

My two favorite parts of the story about this beloved daughter who got healed are 1) the love of Jesus, and 2) the determination and faith of the lady. In those days, anyone with her condition—a continuous flow of blood—was considered unclean. Therefore, they would have been required to live outside the city walls. This lady knew and understood the healing power of Jesus.

She had more than likely heard of the wondrous healing miracles He performed for others. Her mind was set on the fact that, if she could just get to Jesus, her own healing was guaranteed. The first obstacle she had to overcome was getting into the city since her present condition prevented her. After getting into the city and finally locating Jesus, she found that the heavy crowd completely surrounded Him preventing her direct access to Him.

She would have had to have possessed an unusual strength of mind because the long years she suffered from her condition would very likely have caused her to become physically weak, thin, and frail. But she was determined and she strengthened her mind and emotions against every obstacle, not caring what anybody would do or say to her because of her condition. She focused only on Jesus and made her way directly to Him.

When she got close, there were many people tightly surrounding Him. Persistently, she fought her way through this thick crowd of people which included Jesus' twelve disciples. Finally, she was able to reach out and touch the hem of His garment and was instantly and completely healed. Jesus told her that it was her faith that made her well. Many times, people do not receive their miracles because they sit back and wait for it to happen instead of actively seeking the Lord to receive everything He has already promised. Her breakthrough was dependent on her willingness to seek out Jesus and press into Him for her answer. Yours is too!

Psalm 97:5 says, "Mountains melt like wax in the presence of the Lord." Obstacles will fall away one-by-one if you are willing to seek and press into Him. Do whatever it takes to get to Jesus!

CHAPTER 5
MANIFESTING THE POWER OF GOD

Acts 3:1-16 tells the following story: "Now Peter and John went up together to the temple at the hour of prayer, the ninth hour. And a certain man lame from his mother's womb was carried, whom they laid daily at the gate of the temple which is called Beautiful, to ask alms from those who entered the temple; who, seeing Peter and John about to go into the temple, asked for alms. And fixing his eyes on him, with John, Peter said, "Look at us." So he gave them his attention, expecting to receive something from them. Then Peter said, "Silver and gold I do not have, but what I do have I give you: In the name of Jesus Christ of Nazareth, rise up and walk." And he took him by the right hand and lifted him up, and immediately his feet and ankle bones received strength. So he, leaping up, stood and walked and entered the temple with them—walking, leaping, and praising God. And all the people saw him walking and praising God. Then they knew that it was he who sat begging alms at the Beautiful Gate of the temple; and they were filled with wonder and amazement at what had happened to him. Now as the lame man who was healed held on to Peter and John, all the people ran together to them in the porch which is called Solomon's, greatly amazed. So when Peter saw it, he responded to the people: "Men of Israel, why do you marvel at this? Or why look so intently at us, as though by our own power or godliness we had made this man walk? The God of Abraham, Isaac, and Jacob, the God of our fathers, glorified His Servant Jesus, whom you delivered up and denied in the presence of Pilate, when he was determined to let Him go. But you denied the Holy One and the Just, and asked for a murderer to be granted to you, and killed the Prince of life, whom God raised from the dead, of which we are witnesses. And His name, through faith in His name, has made this man strong, whom you see and know. Yes, the faith which comes through Him has given him this perfect soundness in the presence of you all."

We can see here that Peter and John simply took time to stop and talk with the man. That was a big miracle in itself. Most people of that day—and, sadly, also today—would never have taken the time to even stop and acknowledge the crippled man much less engage in a conversation with him. Here was a man who sat right outside the temple gate for years and had never even been into the temple. I wonder what he thought about religious people. Here are these people who went to church every Sunday wearing their nice clothes all dressed up. But they walked right past him, going into the building, never taking him inside with them. Let the same no longer be said of the church of our day. Let us be intentional in loving, inviting, and welcoming people—regardless of their condition, past history, or social and financial status—into the family of God. The world may know that you go to church, but now they need to see you manifest the power of God in your day-to-day life. This means demonstrating both the compassionate, authentic love of Jesus Christ and the explosive, wonder-working power of His Holy Spirit everywhere we go. We are called to live out the examples seen in the book of Acts in our day.

Acts 2:43 says, "Then fear came upon every soul, and many wonders and signs were done through the apostles." Signs and wonders are a mark of an apostolic church or company of people. Acts 4:30 says, "By stretching out Your hand to heal, and that signs and wonders may be done through the name of Your Holy Servant Jesus." There are two major things that can be pulled from this text. The first one is that we can stretch out our hands and pray with extreme faith to see healings and miracles take place; the second one is that we can do so only in the mighty and matchless name of Jesus Christ. We have to be willing to move toward a person or a certain situation when we can sense that there is a great opportunity for a miracle to be performed.

Acts 4:31 says, "And when they had prayed, the place where they were assembled together was shaken; and they were all filled with the Holy Spirit, and they spoke the word of God with boldness." Whenever you are a person of prayer, you will start to walk with a holy boldness. It will be so much easier for you to step out of your comfort zone and speak the word of God to people and over their situations. We must be ready to declare the promises of God over people, over their physical well-being, and over their situations and circumstances. The Holy Spirit will guide and lead us with boldness to present God's word and perform miracles by His power. Signs and wonders release God's people to minister in boldness.

Acts 5:12 says, "And through the hands of the apostles many signs and wonders were done among the people." Signs and wonders touch every person. Acts 14:3 says, "Therefore they stayed there a long time, speaking boldly in the Lord, who was bearing witness to the word of His grace, granting signs and wonders to be done by their hands." One of the biggest reasons for signs, wonders, and miracles are to give testimony to God's word. In this moment in the history of our world, there are so many churches and ministries that are not filled with the Holy Spirit or with the power of God. Therefore, the people in those ministries get confused after they read the Gospels and the book of Acts. They wonder how they can read the Bible and see the wondrous acts of Jesus and His followers, yet see the complete opposite in today's so-called believers and Christian churches and ministries. We must remember what Paul said in 1 Corinthians 4:20: "For the Kingdom of God is not a matter of talk but of power." In Christ, we are called to be people of great authority and power."

1 Corinthians 12:27-28 says, "Now you are the body of Christ, and members individually. And God has appointed these in the church: first apostles." I personally believe the reason that we are seeing so many true apostles rising up today is so that the foundation of God's word might be laid in the church once again. The

mandate of true apostles is to bring the church back to the place where we believe and speak the word of God in boldness and walk in the miracle working power of Jesus Christ. Apostles are always on the cutting edge of what God is doing in a city or region!

Matthew 9:35-36 says, "Then Jesus went about all the cities and villages, teaching in their synagogues, preaching the gospel of the Kingdom, and healing every sickness and every disease among the people. But when he saw the multitudes, he was moved with compassion on them, because they fainted, and were scattered abroad, as sheep having no shepherd." At this specific point in Jesus's ministry, He was preaching all the sermons on the Kingdom and performing great miracles. Then, He had a moment when He looked around at the huge crowd of people all around Him. He then noticed that no one was tending to the spiritual needs of these people properly and on a regular basis. Matthew 9: 37-38 tells us, "Then Jesus said to the disciples, "The harvest truly is plentiful, but the laborers are few. Therefore, pray the Lord of the harvest to send out laborers (workers) into his harvest." Jesus knew that He had to multiply Himself and His efforts to reach the vast amount of people that were drawn to Him in this region and for the days ahead. This is when Jesus began His amazing plan of duplicating Himself and His efforts and imparting divine authority to those that were with Him.

In Matthew 10:1, Jesus gathered His twelve disciples around Him and gave them authority to drive out impure spirits and heal every sickness and disease. Jesus called them to Himself and basically told them that they had watched Him preach and perform signs, wonders, and miracles long enough. Now He wanted to give them authority and access to the power of God. He wanted them to be divinely empowered to go out and preach and teach everything they had heard Him say for they now had the authority to heal all sickness and disease. This was Jesus' way of ensuring that the Gospel would be preached and the world would be reached even after His death and resurrection. We have the same authority that Jesus gave the twelve disciples available to us today. Recognize and begin to walk in it!

John 5:1-5 says, "After this there was a feast of the Jews, and Jesus went up to Jerusalem. Now there is in Jerusalem by the Sheep Gate a pool, which is called in Hebrew, Bethesda, having five porches. In these lay a great multitude of sick people, blind, lame, paralyzed, waiting for the moving of the water. For an angel went down at a certain time into the pool and stirred up the water; then whoever stepped in first, after the stirring of the water, was made well of whatever disease he had. Now a certain man was there who had an infirmity thirty-eight years."

I think that Jesus looked at this man who had this infirmity for so long and likely wondered why he had never tried to get into the water. The man had the answer right before him this whole time and still did nothing about it. We have the word of God that says we can walk in signs, wonders, and miracles and people all around us are still dying prematurely, living in sickness, demon-oppressed, and in need of all types of miracles. As children of God, we know the truth and are called to walk in the authority of His Word. Now it is time to demonstrate the power of God.

John 5:6 says, "When Jesus saw him lying there, and knew that he already had been in that condition a long time, He said to him, "Do you want to be made well?" It almost seems to me like Jesus was almost asking him in disbelief. It was a very plain and straightforward question. When someone has the answer right in front of them, but continues to remain in the same negative condition, it usually means that they have many excuses to justify why they are not well. People tend to overthink and analyze every reason as to why something will not work. In John 5:7, "The sick man answered Him, "Sir, I have no man to put me into the pool when the water is stirred up; but while I am coming, another steps down before me." This man had more than one excuse. Like many people, he blamed others for cutting in front of him and held fast to his claim that nobody would help him. He had one sad story right after another. Then Jesus spoke to him with all authority and power.

John 5:8-9 tells us that "Jesus said to him, "Rise, take up your bed and walk." And immediately the man was made well, took up his bed, and walked!" Jesus told him to GET UP! Sometimes you need to look at somebody and their situation and speak right to the heart of the matter and tell them to get up and go and live the life that God has called and anointed them to live. When we speak the word of God over people, it changes all of their situations and circumstances. We speak forth miracles into the lives of people who are laying right beside their breakthrough. It is time that you enforce the opinion of God over the people that you know in the cities and regions you live in. This is a season for unprecedented breakthroughs and miracles!

When this man was healed, he was free to fulfill his God-given destiny. The healing miracle happened for two reasons. The first one was because Jesus loved him. The second was because this man had a calling from heaven on his life and he sure was not going to complete it laying down. In his previous condition, not only could he not help himself, he certainly was not in a position to help anyone else. By God's merciful grace and miraculous favor, his time of remembrance came and he received his breakthrough. Again, remember, that Kingdom breakthrough is coming to many for Kingdom increase. Remember it is all about God and His Kingdom.

CHAPTER 6
FAITH OR FEAR

It seems that almost every situation and circumstance in life has a faith or fear option. Many times in life we are faced with decisions. It is up to us to choose whether or not we are going to operate out of faith or fear. Far too many times people choose fear over faith, especially when God is trying to change certain things about their life. The years ahead are going to be a time in which the children of God are going to have to make significant Kingdom decisions. We must operate out of the faith realm, fully believing that God will be faithful to do everything He said He would do.

Isaiah 42:9 says, "Behold, the former things are come to pass, and new things do I declare: before they spring forth I tell you of them." The two words that I want to highlight out of this passage are the words former and declare. The word former has four basic one word meanings: first, most, highest, and past. "Now the former things have come to pass." But here is what the word former means when it is broken down. It means the things that we think about first. It also means the things that we think about the most or give the highest regard and greatest priority. But what we must remember is that it refers to things of the past. When we think about our future, many times we tend to insert the former things. But remember that, unless you want history to constantly repeat itself, the former things are in the past and must continue to remain there. Now, the Lord is doing a new thing! So quit allowing your mind to continue to think on the former things first. Quit giving those things the greatest amount of thought and priority in your mind and quit putting them in the highest place. They are of the past and that is exactly where they need to stay—in the past behind you!

Now the word I like the most is the word declare, which simply means "to pronounce the opposite out loud." When you have to make a decision that is going to bring change, you have to be decisive in breaking from the past and moving forward into a new day. Are you going to go back to the former things and allow history to repeat itself, or are you going to stand up and declare that an opposite outcome is going to happen. You will not return to your past failures; you will not make the same mistakes again; you will not be silent any longer; you will no longer fall to the same recurring sin cycle; you are no longer insecure, etc. Declare your God-ordained future over your life. Stand up and pronounce that the opposite is going to happen and now is the time that you will move forward toward the things God has planned for you.

Faith means having complete trust and confidence in God. On the other hand, fear means experiencing unpleasant emotions or anxiety over the outcome of something or fearing danger to someone. Whenever you get a bad doctor's report, do you insert faith or fear to the equation? When a family member gets a bad doctor's report, do you deposit faith or fear into their heart? When you get a bad report about your job, do you deposit faith or fear into your own heart? If you have a prodigal son or daughter who should have been home hours ago and it is late in the night, do not allow yourself to meditate on fearful thoughts. Rather, choose to pull on the faith in you and remind God of His promise that your child would serve Him and fulfill the mighty call on his or her life. Then rest easy knowing the power of the Holy Spirit will draw him or her back.

We must remember Luke 10:19 where Jesus said to His disciples, "Behold, I give you power!" God has given us authority—His authority—which is delegated power! In the days ahead, I feel that there will be greater waves of perversion coming to America. There will be more strategic tricks of the enemy coming at us, so we need to be ready as children of God. Now when I said that, did you respond in faith or fear? We are about to walk into many years of the most powerful signs, wonders, and miracles the world has seen yet. Since there are masses of people who are hurting and broken, there needs to be a great revival of signs, wonders, and miracles. Because of the enormity and seriousness of the need, we are about to enter into an unprecedented season of explosive healing, deliverance, and restoration ministry with a central focus on the life-transforming message of the Gospel of Jesus Christ. We need to have extreme faith because our assignments are going to require that we walk in high levels of authority and power from God.

I hope you remember what Jesus said in John 14:12-14. He said, "Most assuredly, I say to you, he who believes in me, the works that I do he will do also; and greater works than these he will do, because I go to my Father. And whatever you ask in my name, that I will do, that the Father may be glorified in the Son. If you ask anything in my name, I will do it." One day the disciples were probably talking to Jesus about the messages He was preaching, and the miraculous signs and wonders He was performing. They were likely reminiscing about all the devils He cast out in the regions He visited and about all the awesome wonders they had witnessed. Then Jesus said something like, "Guys you think all that is cool? You think what I do is awesome? I am about to go be at the right hand of the Father and, when He sends the Holy Spirit, you are going to do the same things that you have seen Me do. In fact, I love you so much that I am going to let you, as the new body of Christ, do greater works than I have ever done." For the body of Christ to do greater works than Jesus did, we better be ready to walk in signs, wonders, and miracles with extreme authority. When the Holy Spirit moves us toward a certain situation or person, we must operate in extreme faith to see the outcome that God intended.

Matthew 18:18, "Assuredly, I say to you, whatever you bind on earth will be bound in heaven, and whatever you loose on earth will be loosed in heaven." Look at the scripture this way: If someone comes to you bound or handcuffed by the enemy, you would simply pray for them and declare freedom over their life. The handcuffs would open and they would be completely freed from whatever was binding them. Then they would be loosed. Now, as certain as that person is loosed from what used to bind them, you would take the handcuffs and bind the devil in that situation over that person's life. Where they were bound, they are now free. Where the enemy had control, now he has none in that situation over them. We have that power when we call upon the name of the Lord and pray, especially when we earnestly intercede on behalf of others from a place of Christlike love, genuine compassion, and purity of heart.

Matthew 18:19-20, "Again, I say to you that if two of you agree on earth concerning anything that they ask, it will be done for them by My Father in heaven. For where two or three are gathered together in My name, I am there in the midst of them." Remember, whenever a few of us get together to pray, the mighty, miracle working power of the Holy Spirit is right there in the midst of us. So pray with confidence knowing that God has your back!

Ephesians 1:19 in the Passion Translation says, "My prayer for you is that every moment you will experience the measureless power of God made available to you through faith. Then your lives will be an advertisement of the immense power as it works through you." The Apostle Paul is saying here that his earnest prayer and heart is that we will learn to experience the limitless power available to us as children of God. When we exercise our faith, we can see everything that we come in contact with in every atmosphere completely change for the glory of God. The atmosphere at home among our family can be completely shifted by God's power. Our work environment can be changed because of our faith. Our financial situations can experience the limitless power of God. If we have a neighbor or family member who is sick, God's power is more than able to bring about healing. Everything about our day-to-day lives can be changed and the power of God is made available to us to do so.

Ephesians 1:20 in the Passion Translation says, "This is the explosive and mighty resurrection power that was released when God raised Christ from the dead and exalted him to the place of highest honor and supreme authority in the heavenly realm." The same mighty and explosive power that God Himself used to raise Jesus Christ from the dead is available to us. God used this power to raise Jesus up and place Him at His right hand in the highest place of honor. This means, when you speak life over a person or situation, you call it forth all the way up until it is in its rightful place in Christ. When we stand in the authority of God and declare over a thing, we put it in its rightful place. After His resurrection, Jesus' rightful place was not in the tomb any longer. It was at the right hand of the Father. You need to call some things out of the tomb. Begin from today to do so! Be bold in declaring the manifestation of miracles with this mighty power! Command situations and circumstances to get into alignment with the word of God!

Ephesians 6:10 in the Passion Translation says, "Now finally, my beloved ones, be supernaturally infused with strength through your life-union with the Lord Jesus. Stand victorious with the force of His explosive power flowing in and through you." You must understand that you have got to take a stand for the things that God has placed in your heart. God is asking every one of us to not budge an inch when it comes to the truth of His word. God does an extreme work in us in our private prayer times and in our secret place of devotion. Then, when we go out in public, He is able to flow freely and powerfully through us. God made us to where we can be supernaturally filled with divine power when we call upon the name of Jesus. That explosive power can be used and manifested when you declare the will of God over somebody's life or in a particular situation. You have the power to call people's lives, situations and circumstances into proper alignment.

Ephesians 1:18 says, "The eyes of your understanding being enlightened; that you may know what is the hope of His calling, what are the riches of the glory of His inheritance in the saints." We need to be enlightened so that we can understand how much is available to us in Christ. If we could see deeply into the spirit realm, we would understand that there is more available to us than anybody can fathom or than has even been tapped into. The Lord has a powerful inheritance for His children. Many people fail to walk in this inheritance because they simply refuse to identify with the authority and power God has given us. The inheritance that God has for His children consists of many things like peace, grace, mercy, health, joy, prosperity, etc. The list goes on and on.

In the natural, the body is made up of many different parts, but the head controls the body. The same is true in the spiritual realm. Jesus Christ is the head and we, the Church, are His body. Where the head tells us to go, we go; and when we go, we go in POWER! God has so much stored up for His people. God needs the body of Christ to be complete and made whole so we do not limp or stagger into battle every day. Rather, through Christ, we go in with hearts and minds full of the promises of God. In this frame of mind, we are ready to impact all of our surroundings and transform every atmosphere that we walk into with the presence of God. We have the power to do that, you know!

Ephesians 3:19 says, "To know the love of Christ which passes knowledge; that you may be filled with all the fullness of God." The love and power of Christ is something that you must experience for yourself. You cannot just read about it and think you truly know it. It is so much more than just head knowledge. God wants us to be completely filled and flooded with all of His fullness. You are supposed to live a life of overflowing love, joy, peace, favor, increase, and blessings. I want all that God has for me spiritually, physically, emotionally, financially, and mentally; and I want the same for you!

Ephesians 3:20 says, "Now to Him who is able to do exceedingly abundantly above all that we ask or think, according to the power that works in us." When we truly tap into the Kingdom of God and understand how it operates, we will have exceedingly, abundantly, above all that we can ask for in the place of prayer. We will have more than we can even think about. It is all according to the authority and power level that we have working inside of us. You see, you cannot think on the natural realm with earthly understanding and fully grasp this text to the fullest. But when you think with God's Kingdom mindset, this scripture makes complete sense. You do not pray for yourself personally to be blessed with earthly things as the main point of focus in your walk with God. You focus rather on the things of the Kingdom and strongly desire that God would use you to help orchestrate His divine plan for the earth.

CHAPTER 7
CALLED TO MIRACLES

Many times, people believe the lie that miracles are not for them. Numerous people have told me that there is no way they can ever be used of God at such a great measure. Too often they have bought into the lie that they have been overlooked. I am here to speak a word of encouragement to those of you that feel like you are underqualified, overlooked, misunderstood, or that no one has ever taken you seriously. You are the exact ones that God desires to use in this hour! Just take a look at what the scriptures say in 1 Corinthians 1:26-31 of the New Life version and be encouraged. "Christian brothers, think who you were when the Lord called you. Not many of you were wise or powerful or born into the family of leaders of a country. But God has chosen what the world calls foolish to shame the wise. He has chosen what the world calls weak to shame what is strong. God has chosen what is weak and foolish of the world, what is hated and not known, to destroy the things the world trusts in. In that way, no man can be proud as he stands before God. God Himself made the way so you can have new life through Christ Jesus. God gave us Christ to be our wisdom. Christ made us right with God and set us apart for God and made us holy. Christ bought us with His blood and made us free from our sins. It is as the Holy Writings say, "If anyone is going to be proud of anything, he should be proud of the Lord."

Back in Jesus' time, if you were going to serve as a priest in the temple, you had to be chosen at the age of twelve. This means that a Rabbi had to come and personally invite you to serve as an intern under him and would teach and train you for a life devoted to ministry. I do not recall any of the original twelve disciples being raised up by a Rabbi. I do remember, however, that a few of them were fishermen and there was one tax collector in the bunch. You see, the twelve people Jesus chose to turn the world upside down had vocational jobs. As far as we can tell from the scriptures, they had no formal training and clearly had not been selected by any Rabbi of that day for the honored position of an intern or trainee. But they were chosen by Jesus to be His own disciples and specially selected helpers in His ministry that changed the history of all of mankind as we know it. Though they may have been overlooked by the bigshots of their day, they were ultimately chosen as first-round draft picks for service and discipleship in the most monumental ministry team in all of time and eternity. So never let the enemy or society tell you that you are not capable of carrying out the work of God. Just when you feel people have counted you out, God has reserved something special in store for you.

God is looking for people with a willing heart and a wholehearted YES in their spirit. Jesus took these twelve ordinary men and gave them extraordinary authority and power. Luke 9:1, "And he called the twelve together and gave them power and authority over all demons and to cure diseases." You have the exact same power and authority available to you. Yes, that is right, you secretary, firemen, stay-at-home mom, teacher, factory worker, etc.! Wherever the Lord has you located, you have the power and authority in Christ Jesus to manifest the Kingdom of God and demonstrate signs, wonders, and miracles to the world around you!

Whether you are at home with your family, at work, school, or a family reunion, always remember that you may be the very one God wants to use in a certain situation to bring life to someone. You may speak a prophetic word over someone's life or grab their hand and say a simple prayer that will shake all of heaven and earth. Remember you have authority to change people's lives by the prayers you pray and the words you declare. Someone's miracle may be in your mouth. Luke 10:19 says, "Behold, I have given to you power to tread on serpents and scorpions, and over all the power of the enemy: and nothing shall by any means hurt you."

Years ago, my wife and I were living outside of Houston working for an internship and conference ministry. One morning, I was headed to the church to go to a meeting. Right before I left, my wife's hip popped out of its socket and she grabbed her side and fell to the ground. I picked her up and placed her on the bed. She was crying and talking about how much pain she was in. At that time, we did not have any insurance or money to pay for doctor bills and I did not know what we were going to do about her care. It is easy to have a lot of faith when you do not have insurance or money. In such situations, you have no other option but to trust in the Lord. I remember crying out to God saying "Lord, heal my wife! Please touch her right now! We do not have the money or insurance to cover any medical bills. God, You are our only option! We need You now!" A few minutes later, my wife encouraged me to just go to the meeting. She said, "I will lay here for little while and you can come back and check on me." After she assured me she would be alright in the meantime, I left and went to the meeting. Later, when I walked out of the meeting, I saw my wife jogging down the hall of the church. She smiled and said, "I'm fine," as she went on about her business. These were some of the ways God used to teach us about His miracle working power in times of emergency where we had to have Him move and intervene on our behalf.

I also recall another incident when I was in my young twenties that the Lord used to build my faith. I had just met my wife and started working out really hard to try to get bigger muscles to impress her. During this season of pushing myself way too hard physically, I developed knots on my lower stomach. One night in a prayer meeting, I was in obvious pain and two intercessors came over to me and asked me what was wrong. I told them about the knots on my stomach and they said, "Let us see." I began to refuse and said "No, you are not going to lift my shirt up. Thankfully, one of the intercessors pulled my shirt up anyhow, saw the knots and laid hands on them. Right before my eyes those knots on the lower part of my stomach dissolved completely and the skin color went back to normal. Then those ladies just went back to drinking their coffee and praying to Jesus.

Another personal story is of a time when we were doing a conference and the Lord laid it on my heart to call people up for healing. I remember three young men came up to one side of the platform. One gentleman was wearing a boot cast and, as we prayed, he took the boot cast off, lifted it in the air, and started to dance around. The other two young men both had surgery scheduled, one for his knee and one for an ankle. God miraculously touched and healed both of these young men and both of them ended up cancelling their surgeries. The funny thing about it was that I was in a boot cast myself and my doctor told me I had to have three screws in my foot because it was broken about ninety percent in half. The Lord spoke to me about taking off my boot cast and dancing before Him in the altar space at the front. I did just as the Lord instructed me to and ended up never needing the surgery the doctor said I absolutely had to have.

Matthew 28:18-20 says, "Jesus came to the disciples and said "All power is given to me in heaven and in earth. Now go ye therefore and teach all nations, baptizing them in the name of the Father, the Son and the Holy Ghost; teaching them to observe all things whatsoever I have commanded you; and I am with you always, even unto the end of the world." The Lord has called and instructed us to go out and preach the word of God with boldness and move in signs, wonders, and miracles. The church today needs to see the power of God. The church of America has yet to see the bible lived out as the true, active word that it is. The enemy is not just fighting the church of today; he is also trying to destroy the church of tomorrow. THE DEVIL IS TRYING TO DESTROY THE NEXT GENERATION!

John 10:10 says, "The devil comes to steal, to kill and destroy, but I am coming that you will have life and life more abundantly." The enemy has tried to come in and steal people's health, finances, marriages, dreams, relationships, jobs, etc. The list goes on and on. He has tried to kill the children of God and destroy them in every way possible. But the great news, my friends, is that the Lord is coming to give us life and that life more abundantly. So many people could be affected in a great measure if you would step up and step out, dare to believe God's word, and be a living demonstration of His power. Ephesians 6:10 says, "Finally, my brethren be strong in the Lord and in the power of his might."

One of my favorite miracle stories to share is about a nineteen year-old girl who got out of her wheelchair. My wife and I had travelled with our children and were preaching for a pastor friend of ours. As I was speaking, I did not have any Scriptures about miracles and had not planned to speak on the subject. In the middle of the message, the Spirit of God led me to speak on miracles for seven minutes. At the end of the service a few people gave their lives to the Lord, and a few more rededicated their lives back to Him. I had been praying for some people on one side of the sanctuary, but then the pastor called me back up toward the front. A young man brought a young girl up in her wheelchair and we were asked to pray for her healing. At that time, she had been involved in an accident and had no use of her legs nor any feeling in them.

When I was about to pray, I felt the Lord say He wanted to do this healing step-by-step so the people could see her restoration right in front of their eyes. I remember asking all the people of faith to gather around. There were about seventy people in all and I do not believe there was a dry eye in the house. The first thing I declared was, "In the name of Jesus, I pray that you can feel your legs." Right then, the young girl said, "My legs have a tingly feeling; I can feel my legs!" The entire place erupted with praise. I quickly said, "Let's thank the Lord for that, but God's about to do more." Then I said, "I pray in the name of Jesus that you can move your legs." This young girl started to move her legs. The church took its praise and thanksgiving to God to another level. Then I remember asking the young man, who was also her fiancé, and the pastor to get alongside her and help her up. They stood on each side of her and helped her to her feet in a pair of three-inch stilettos. While they held her steady by her arms, she took about five steps, then asked to sit back down.

Two weeks later the pastor texted me to share that the young lady was now walking using a cane. Two weeks after that she was walking on her own. A year later, the pastor sent me a picture of her dancing at her wedding. I went back to preach at that church about two years after that. A young man that traveled with me on that particular preaching trip used to work in the same physical therapy center that had been working with this young lady after the accident. He said to me, "I remember that young girl over there. I remember the doctors had said that girl has absolutely no chance of ever walking again." I then told him the story of how God miraculously healed her in the church service two years earlier. Listen, my friends, God will interrupt your message, your life, or anything that you are doing when you are willing to allow him to use you for miracles. Be open to this, because your obedience could be the doorway to major, life-altering change and breakthrough in the lives of others.

Kingdom people are about to receive divine increase that is designed for Kingdom purposes! The increase that is coming is for Kingdom breakthrough. When you use the increase God blesses you with for Kingdom purposes, the flow never stops. It becomes a way of life! I'm talking about mental, emotional, spiritual, financial, and relational increase! One of the ways the enemy hinders your assignment is by diverting your attention! Do not give your time and energy to wrong people, voices, or thoughts. Sometimes the breakthrough we have been waiting for happens when we allow God to break through in our thinking! Remember, Kingdom breakthrough is coming for Kingdom increase.

CHAPTER 8
A RENEWED MIND

So many people need to have their mind completely restored and renewed. The majority of people were not raised up to understand the concept of breakthroughs, or of signs, wonders, and miracles. It is amazing how many people do not actually believe the word of God is true. A lot of people say they believe it is true, but if they do not walk in signs, wonders, and miracles, their actions speak for them. We need a renewed mind to understand the Kingdom of God and the fullness that is available to us in it. Bill Johnson said, "We will know when our mind is truly renewed because the impossible will look logical."

Whenever I get a chance to talk to someone and have a personal conversation with them, I can usually tell very quickly how well their mind is developed toward the things of God. There are many believers who are very emotionally unstable and cannot mentally handle a whole lot of warfare. There are numerous people I know that can walk through hard times in warfare and hardly even be fazed. Then there are others that can have the smallest, little attack come their way and it completely knocks them out of everything they are doing. We have to learn to remember the prophetic words God has spoken over our lives and trust in the written word of God. We must understand the depth of power contained in the Scriptures.

So many people have heard the Lord speak to them directly about their destiny, purpose, and God dreams over their life. Many people know the direction in which God has called them to walk. As long as we stay focused on the Kingdom of God and the things of His Spirit, we will continue to press toward the mark He is leading us toward. Unfortunately, many times people can have one little obstacle come in their way and it completely gets them off course. God wants to renew the minds of His saints so we can be battle ready and battle tested. God needs people to be strong in their spirit and strong in their mind. We cannot give in to fear, anxiety, or insecurities when the enemy brings them our way. We must stay focused on the Lord and the words He has spoken over our lives.

James 1:8 says, "A double-minded man is unstable in all his ways." Far too many times I have seen people who receive an impartation from God and are running strong after the Lord and the things He has for them suddenly fall off course because they were double-minded. The word says that these kinds of people are double-minded and unstable in all of their ways. These people are very scary and toxic individuals to associate with because you will start to depend on them and rely on them but as soon as an attack comes, they completely bail out of the project they were co-laboring on. This is because many people have not developed a strong and steadfast mind in Christ.

Every one of us has a breathtaking purpose from God for our life. The enemy knows this and is going to throw every trick in the book at us to try to knock us all off our mark. I have seen too many people give up because one person spoke a negative word of criticism over their life concerning the project they were working on. Whenever God elevates you to a higher level or dimension, you do not have to find your critics. They will find you and you will know who they are. You must understand that critics are angry, jealous, and bitter because they are watching others do what they were called to do, but refused to step out in faith to do.

The reason that sometimes strangers will support you more than the people who have known you, is because the people that have known you for a long time sometimes have a tough time accepting who you have become and the great things the Lord has been doing in and through you. They may be from the same city or region, but they remained stuck in the same place while you moved on and continue to grow in the things of God. Never let the words of critics keep you from moving on with the Lord. Strong-minded believers have to identify the source of the criticism and then separate the person from the spirit fueling them to shoot those fiery darts of discouragement at you. Make a conscious decision to forgive them in advance. The Lord Himself will ultimately step in to vindicate you eventually, but in the meantime, your heart is kept free to continue to walk in God's love and power unhindered.

Romans 12:2 says, "Do not be conformed to this world, but be transformed by the renewing of your mind, that you may prove what is that good and acceptable and perfect will of God." We can never let the words of critics and haters shape our life. We must allow the word of God alone to shape our life. When your mind is renewed and you know the voice of your heavenly Father, no earthly voice can get you off the road to your destiny. When you know the perfect will of God for your life, you will stay straight on that target no matter what. Ephesians 4:23-24 says, "Be renewed in the spirit of your mind, and that you put on the new man which was created according to God, and true righteousness and holiness."

Proverbs 3:5-6 says, "Trust in the Lord with all your heart, and lean not on your own understanding; In all your ways acknowledge Him, And He shall direct your paths." Whenever you read the word heart in the bible, remember it is divided into the spirit and the soul and that the soul is divided into the mind and the emotions. When the verse says, "Lean not on your own understanding," it is encouraging you to not let your mind and emotions lead you astray, but rather to always follow after the leading of the Holy Spirit. This is why when the scripture says "in all your ways" it means in every single thing that you do. When your spirit, mind, and emotions are all focused on the same goal or project, you will surely hit your mark. This is because having a renewed mind demonstrates clearly that your spirit is willing, your mind is focused, and your emotions are intact. Therefore, you are stable and standing on a firm foundation, the foundation of Jesus Christ.

Hebrews 4:12 says, "For the word of God is living and powerful, and sharper than any two-edged sword, piercing even to the division of soul and spirit, and of joints and marrow, and is a discerner of the thoughts and intents of the heart." When I was young, many times hanging out with my grandparents, I would hear the old-timers say, "My heart is divided on this situation." This means, "My spirit is telling me one thing but the compassionate side of me is wanting to do something else." Over the years, I have learned to always follow the leading of the Holy Spirit.

Matthew 22:37 says, "Jesus said to them, "You shall love the Lord God with all of your heart, with all of your soul, and all of your mind." The heart, soul, and mind represent the whole body. Our lives are called to be effective witnesses for Christ. When our body is whole and complete, we will be better able to maximize our efforts for God. 1 Corinthians 2:16 says, "For who has known the mind of the Lord that he may instruct him? But we have the mind of Christ." We should start to think like Christ. When we allow God to renew our mind, we will start to see our lives change in powerful ways. Watch for this in your own life. The people closest to you will start to comment about how you are acting differently and reacting to things with different mannerisms. Ask God in your prayer time to bring clarity to your mind in your decision-making process.

2 Timothy 1:7 says, "Therefore, I remind you to stir up the gift of God which is in you by the laying on of hands, for God has not given us the spirit of fear, but of power and love and of a sound mind." This scripture tells us that God's Spirit does not give fear, anxiety, insecurity, etc., but rather power, love, and a sound mind. We must remember that when the Lord wants us to step out to be effective witnesses moving in the authority and power He has given us, oftentimes fear tries to creep in. Remember where the fear comes from and that it is not from the Spirit of God. Rise up and rebuke the spirit of fear from your life and move forward boldly by faith in being the hands, feet, and mouthpiece of God. Never let anxiety attack you. Rebuke it and speak peace over your life. Never allow insecurity to hold you back. Declare that your mind is steadfastly set on God and the things He has for you. Start to quote promises from the scriptures over your life.

Philippians 4:6-8 says, "Be anxious for nothing, but in everything by prayer and supplication, with Thanksgiving, let your requests be made known to God. And the peace of God, which surpasses all understanding, will guard your hearts and minds through Christ Jesus. Finally brethren, whatever things are true, whatever things are noble, whatever things are just, whatever things are pure, whatever things are lovely, whatever things are of good report, if there is any virtue and if there is anything praiseworthy, meditate on these things." When we live a life devoted to God and spend a good portion of our time in the secret place of prayer, this will drive anxiety and fear far away from the door of our heart. When you keep your mind steadfastly on the Lord and are constantly receiving fresh impartations from Him, and when you stay current with what God is saying over your life, your mind and heart will be at peace no matter what season or circumstance your life is in. We must do our part to keep our minds focused on all of the keywords mentioned in verse eight. Do not allow your mind to veer off or give attention to any idle seed that someone tries to plan in your heart. A renewed heart and mind with the fresh touch of God upon it can overcome and accomplish anything.

Psalm 119:9-11 says, "How can a young man cleanse his way? By taking heed according to your word. With my whole heart I have sought after you, O let me not wander from your commandments. Your word I have hidden in my heart, that I might not sin against you." The closer you draw to God every day, the harder it will be for you to fall away. Reading the word daily and staying in prayer will keep the Lord's commandments before you. As long as you keep your mind freshly renewed in the Lord, it will always remain sharp and precise as you allow the Holy Spirit to guide you. There is nothing more rewarding and fun in this life as living a life with your whole heart focused on God and the things that He has for you. What would your life be like if every aspect of it was pointed in the direction God intends for you to go. There would be no limit to the success God will bring in your direction.

Colossians 3:16 says, "The manifestation of God will be in you richly, filling you with all wisdom. Apply the Scriptures as you teach and instruct one another with psalms, festive praise, and with prophetic songs given spontaneously by the Spirit. As the foundation of grace overflows with in you singing to God with all of your hearts." My friends, there is no limit to how powerfully God can use you when you allow His Holy Spirit to guide, lead, and direct you.

When we fully give our lives to the Holy Spirit and give Him free reign to pull things from us that we do not need and impart wisdom and knowledge that we do need, He will be able to use us in mighty ways. Every believer dreams of living the life God created them to live to the absolute fullness. How about beginning from this moment to allow the Holy Spirit to renew your spirit, mind, and emotions, so you can start living that life today. There are so many people around you that will benefit from your life greatly when you are hitting on all cylinders.

Whenever you get a word from God, you have to settle in your heart that it will come to pass. Do not allow your mind to overanalyze and overthink every situation concerning this word. Never allow your emotions to get out of line or begin to go off your feelings. Whenever you get a powerful direction or word from the Lord, the enemy will commit himself and his demons to fighting you in basically every single area of your life to try to get that word stopped and aborted. Let's look at one small part of the Apostle Paul's life.

We see in Acts 23:11 that the Lord stood near Paul and said, "Take courage! As you have testified about me in Jerusalem, so you must also testify in Rome." Now the word of the Lord was that Paul was going to go to Rome and that he would testify about the goodness of God there. So you can bet over the next few chapters, we are about to read about the enemy's attempts to stop Paul in every way possible. The only way the devil can stop you is if you quit moving forward. This is why it is so important to have your spirit, mind, and emotions all pointed in the same direction.

Now at that particular time, Paul was a prisoner on a ship full of prisoners. A terrible storm built up around the ship that Paul was being transported on. The guards were afraid that if there was a shipwreck and some of the prisoners escaped, they would lose their own lives. Back then, it was the custom of the guards to kill all the prisoners rather than let them escape because of a storm. Acts 27:42-43 tells us, "And the soldiers plan was to kill all the prisoners, lest any of them swim away and escape; but the Centurion wanted to save Paul and kept them from their purpose." In essence, this Centurion stood up and said, "You can kill whoever you want to kill, but this one guy right here, you are not going to be able to touch him." So as the ship was being torn apart, everybody jumped in the freezing water and started to swim to the island of Malta. When they got to the shore it was very cold. They had just gotten out of the cold water and, before that, had been fighting to stay afloat on a ship tossed to and fro by the waves of the storm until it was destroyed; not to mention that they were famished and extremely hungry. So, basically, they were tired, weary, hungry, and completely worn out.

Acts 28:2-3 says, "And the natives showed us unusual kindness, for they kindled a fire and made us welcome, because it'd became cold. But when Paul had gathered a bundle of sticks and laid them on the fire, a Viper came out because of the heat, and fastened upon Paul's hand." Just when the Apostle Paul thought he was finally going to get a little warmth and hopefully something to eat, a viper fastened to his hand. Now it did not just bite him, it fastened upon him which means it latched on and hung from his hand. My friends, let me take a moment here to stop and encourage all of you that no matter how bad things get, never ever count God out of the situation. John 10:10 tells us that, "The enemy came to kill, steal and destroy, but God came to give life and life more abundantly."

Acts 28:4-5, "The natives assumed he must be a murderer because this happened. But when he shook off the creature into the fire and had suffered no harm, they respected him greatly and changed their minds and said he must be a God." One minute everybody was accusing Paul of so many things because this happened to him, but when he stood there in honor and integrity and just shook off the attack, they claimed he must be a God.

Whenever the enemy fights you at every turn and presses you sorely, you can learn to stand with a sound mind and be full of God's Spirit. When you show strong character and integrity, people will see how you withstand the attacks of the enemy. You will eventually gain their respect which will give you an open door to speak into their life. Paul now had influence to speak into the lives of the people of the island of Malta even though he had not even spoken a single word.

This is the power of having a renewed mind. Most people would have fallen to the ground when the viper fastened on them and said, "Lord, I can't take anymore. I have gone through a shipwreck in bad weather, had to swim in cold water, and I'm just plain tired!" They would feel perfectly justified in throwing a fit. Not the apostle Paul though. He stood with integrity in front of all his accusers. Just like the apostle Paul, you never have to explain yourself. The best response to your critics is godly success. Keep a strong mind and stay focused on God. What you have been through should have killed you, but people watched you survive! Hang on; your Kingdom increase is coming for great Kingdom breakthrough!

CHAPTER 9
DESTROYING ROADBLOCKS

Have you ever felt like every single time you get ready to make an advancement in life you begin to hit roadblocks. Maybe it seems like you are about to run the hundred-yard dash, but when the gun goes off, it turns into the hundred and ten-yard dash, ...with hurdles! It may seem that, like the children of Israel, you were only supposed to go on an eleven day journey, but it has been forty years. The enemy, the thief, the devil are some of the ways the scriptures refer to the forever loser. He will always try to kill, abort, destroy, intimidate, or frustrate everything you try to do for God. John 10:10 says, "The thief (devil) comes to kill, steal, and destroy. I have come to give you life and life more abundantly."

When these things occur, learn to rejoice! It takes the wind out of the enemy's sails. Choose instead to remain laser focused on God and He will get you through every one of these tests, trials, and tribulations. The constant attacks can either advance or detour us. We need to understand that advancement in the Kingdom of God usually comes after the enemy's attacks. The harsher the attack, the greater the Kingdom advancement!

Now let's look at the four keywords in John 10:10. The word kill means to cause death to a person or a living thing. When you receive a word straight from the Lord or a prophetic word, that word is alive but the enemy wants to kill it. The word steal means to take something without permission with the intention of never returning it. The thief has no right to take anything from you. When he takes something from you, you have to tell your heavenly Father and go get it back. In the name of Jesus, the devil is through stealing from God's people any longer! The word destroy means to put an end to the existence of something or to cause ruin physically, emotionally, or spiritually. The devil wants to bring destruction in every area of your life especially to all your relationships and existing projects. The main problem for him, though, is that his words have no power over that which God has called, blessed, and spoken favor and increase into. God's word trumps the devil's word a hundred percent of the time!

Now let's get to the word I like the best in this particular scripture and that is the word abundantly! The word abundantly means in large, plenty, or extreme quantities. So every area the devil tries to kill, steal, and destroy are the exact same areas in which God wants to restore and bring large quantities of overflow. God wants to give us plenty in every area we need it and add extreme measures of His blessings to our lives. I will believe the report of the Lord all the days of my life. Far too many people have wasted enough of their life and time worrying about the attacks, schemes, and plans of the devil when God has an extremely abundant life full of breakthrough waiting for them. Now is the time for you to start walking in the fullness of the powerful and heavily anointed words God has spoken over your life.

You have to quit believing the lies of the enemy, negative people, critics, and some family members and so call friends. Believe me when I tell you that you are highly favored and blessed. You are about to destroy the roadblocks that have stood in your way and experience mighty breakthroughs and a life full of miracles. Sometimes it starts with allowing God to renew your mind. There are many people in life who have been dealt a much worse hand than you and they are living a fruitful, fun, productive life for God. "Why?" you may ask. Because they simply choose to. If your life is not where you want it to be, quit blaming others, your circumstances, and situations and start changing things by the power of God and prayer. You have to declare the word of the Lord over your life every single day.

Have you ever thought to yourself that there has got to be more to life than what I'm getting out of it? That is because there truly is, my friend. God never sends anyone to earth without an amazing destiny or purpose placed upon their life. This is why sometimes you feel the Holy Spirit pulling you toward him. Drawing you toward the dreams He has for you.

Hebrews 11:6, "But without faith it is impossible to please him, for he who comes to God must believe that he is and that He is a rewarder of those who diligently seek him." Sometimes we have to get out of our stale routine and aggressively seek the Lord. The word plainly says that God will reward those that diligently seek him. The word does not say that He will reward those that hit their snooze button four times instead of getting up to spend time with God. When you are full of the power of God and you know your purpose and destiny, you will not hit the snooze button. You will go to bed at night with the next morning on your mind.

I recently read an article about what successful people all have in common. One of the most important things is that successful people—those who are getting the most out of life—have a morning routine that makes them more effective in every area of life. Let me use myself as an example to encourage you. Personally, I am working on a lot of projects right now, but last week I woke up at 3:30 AM, 4:30 AM, 5 AM twice, and slept in one day to 5:30 AM. Why? Because I have something that God has put in my spirit and I am going hard after it.

The first thing I do every morning is go to the place of prayer. Seriously, I walk right past the coffee pot every morning and go to the place of prayer even before I get my cup of coffee. Sometimes I am up two hours before the coffeepot even goes off. James 4:7-8 says, "Therefore Submit to God, Resist the devil and he will flee from you. Draw near to God and he will draw near to you." Submitting to God is the first and most important thing you will do when you commit your life on this journey with him. The devil will eventually flee because he's tired of coming at somebody who is grounded and rooted in the things of God with a firm foundation. Verse eight assure us that if we draw near to the Lord, He is going to draw near to us. The closer you get to God, the more you will understand about yourself. This is where insecurities fade away.

Jeremiah 29:11 says, "For I know the thoughts that I think toward you says the Lord, thoughts of peace and not of evil, to give you a hope and a future." When you can get this Scripture down in your spirit, it will change your life and transform the way you think about life in general. You must remember this: Never think God has a bad thought or motive toward you! When you realize that God's plan is to give you a hope and a powerful future in Him, it will change the way you think. Sometimes you might just need to ask God to show you what He thinks about you or what He is saying over your life. Remember, God's word assures you that He has already planned a great end to your story!

How do you see your ending? This struggle and strategic attack from the enemy can actually help to advance you! It does not matter what you are going through. God has an amazing plan to get you to the end of this journey that you are on. We might not get to pick the tests that we go through, but our reactions and responses can determine whether or not we finish our assignment in life and pass with flying colors.

Jeremiah 29:12-13 says, "Then you will call upon me and go and pray to me, and I will listen to you. And you will seek me and find me, when you search for me with all of your heart." The Lord is saying that when you call upon Him, He will be there listening. God is a great Father who always listens to His children when they communicate with Him. The Lord says when you seek after Him, you will find Him when you search for Him with all of your heart—spirit, mind, and emotion.

When we seek God on a daily basis, we will make sure that we hit the mark for the end result that God has for us. Always remember that God created you with the end mark in mind. If you are still breathing, He still has a great plan for your life!

Isaiah 55:9 says, "For as the heavens are higher than the earth, So are My ways higher than your ways, And My thoughts than your thoughts." Whenever we are going through difficult circumstances, we must always remember to ask the Lord for wisdom on how to get through the test. Never worry if you fail a test. God doesn't fail His children. He only gives retakes. Sometimes you may not see a way out, but this is when you must ask God to show up and give you wisdom and revelation far beyond your understanding. Like any good father, the Lord will speak to you and help you make sense of everything you are going through. You have to learn how to think HIGHER!!!

Matthew 6:33 says, "Seek First the Kingdom of God and his righteousness, and all these things shall be added unto you." The most important thing we can do is seek the Lord daily, building and strengthening our relationship with Him. Again, the most important thing we will ever do is keep a consistent, private, secret place of prayer time with God. It is absolutely important that we remain steadfast in Christ and become students of His word.

Titus 2:1 says, "As for you, speak the things which are proper for sound doctrine." When we know the word of God and hear the voice of God on a regular basis, no crazy fly by night doctrine, fad, or trend will get us off course. We will stay steadfast on the path on which the Lord has put us. On this path, we will be able to destroy, jump over, or run around any roadblock set in our way. Just as in Psalm 97:5, they will all have to melt like wax in the presence of the Lord. God does not want you to be bound emotionally and mentally nor oppressed and depressed, etc. God wants you to be completely and permanently free!

1 Corinthians 13:11 says, "When I was a child, I spoke as a child, I understood as a child, I thought as a child. But when I became an adult I put away childish things." Some of the biggest roadblocks in life may be the way you speak, process situations, and think about things. So let's do some self-evaluation by asking yourself and honestly answering the following questions concerning your speech. Whenever you are upset at someone or at certain circumstances in your life, how do you speak about that person or situation? What words do you speak over your own life? How do you speak over your job, ministry, or business? What are the words that come out of your mouth about your family and friends? Are you speaking as a child or as a mature believer in Christ?

The next set of questions to honestly ask your-self have to do with your thought life. What does your thought process look like? If someone close to you says some very harmful and damaging words to you, do you accept those words and harbor them in your heart or are you quick to forgive and release? Do you hold it against them for many years or are you able to look at where they came from and assess the situation of that person's life and move on, never letting their negative words affect you? My friends, how you process things internally is a huge determining factor of how you would respond to words and situations that come your way. Do you process as a child or respond as a mature be-liever in Christ?

Again, honestly ask yourself what your thought pro-cess looks like. Do you over analyze everything? Do you tend to think yourself right out of the joy and peace God wants you to experience in your life? Do you think as a child over areas and circumstances in your life or is your outlook that of a mature believer in Christ? Children will get upset and cry about something while adults will think about the situation for a moment, react properly, and then move on. It is time that some people move on past the roadblocks they have currently allowed to take up space in their mind. Move on toward the divine des-tiny God has for you.

When someone attacks you or says something neg-ative, it is over after they say it. How do you choose to speak about that situation? How do you understand or think about it afterwards? How do you respond when you are let go from a job or done wrong by friends? After it happens, make up in your mind that it is over and purpose to move on in your heart, mind, and emotions! Move Forward! When we truly understand that everything we go through can and will make us stronger, we will start to speak differently about things. We will better understand why some things happen and begin to think differently about them. Romans 8:28 tells us, "And we know that for those who love God, all things work together for good, for those who are called according to his purpose."

Proverbs 18:21 tells us that "Death and life are in the Power of the tongue." Remember you do not have to speak out of your mouth everything that your mind is thinking. We should be very wise about the words that we allow to come out of our mouth. In Matthew 12:34 Jesus says, "You brood of vipers! How can you speak good, when you are evil? For out of the abundance of the heart the mouth speaks." Seriously, some of us have got to train our mouths not to say everything we think about. Just because it comes across our mind doesn't mean it has to come across our lips. James 3:2 says, "For we all stumble in many things, but if we do not stumble in our words, we would be perfect." Always allow the Holy Spirit to help you control your words and thoughts. Proverbs 4:7 puts it very helpfully by saying, "Wisdom is the principal thing, therefore get wisdom. And in all your getting, get understanding."

CHAPTER 10
THE KINGDOM OF GOD

Over the past few weeks, I have been seeking the Lord at a very deep level. I have really been leaning strongly on three specific verses. Jeremiah 29:13, "You will seek me and find me when you seek me with all your heart;" Proverbs 8:17, "I love those who love me, and those who seek me find me;" and Hebrews 11:6, "Now without faith it is impossible to please God, for whoever comes to him must believe that he exists and that he rewards those who diligently search for him." I have been diligently seeking the Lord for wisdom and answers on why we do not see more breakthrough and miracles in the Church in America. I remember one of my favorite quotes by Leonard Ravenhill: "One of these days somebody will pick up the Book of God, read it, believe it, and then the rest of us will be embarrassed." This made me start digging into the word of God more than usual because I am convinced that every answer can be found in the Bible.

For many years I have cried out for revival in my life, personally, and for the cities and churches where I have been a part. In my prayer times, I keep repeating a prayer that I heard Pastor John Kilpatrick pray years ago during the Brownsville revival, "God there has to be more". With every ounce and fiber of my being, I have been saying, "God there has to be more than what we are seeing and

I will give the rest of my life to serve and seek you for everything you have for us."

So I started focusing in on reading the four Gospels—Matthew, Mark, Luke, and John—and the book of Acts. Studying these five books of the Bible in depth brought me to some very powerful questions. I studied these intensively in the scriptures and answered my own questions. Why do these books talk so much about the Kingdom of God? Did you know that these five books of the bible never really tell us to pray for the sick but, rather, command us to heal the sick?

A little over 500 years ago, Martin Luther—the great reformer—would go to church and then come home and read the bible. He was able to see clearly that the church of his day was in great error. Martin Luther would get so frustrated that he would challenge the church officials. Because of his love and in-depth study of the word, he knew there was so much more to a relationship and walk with God than they were teaching in the church of his day. Today, I feel the exact same way. There is so much power available to us that we are not even tapping into. In this day and time, my friends, we have to have more than a revival. We must have the very manifestation of the Kingdom of God.

Recently, I had a life changing conversation with the Lord late one night. I was praying and simply told the Lord, "You know I have been crying out for revival in my city and region for many years." I felt the Lord respond to me so passionately saying, "But you have even prayed a greater prayer: that I would send a revival that would be sustained in the geographical location in which I have planted you." Then the Lord showed me that what He desires to do is train, equip, and use me to establish the Kingdom of God wherever He sends me.

A few months back, I had numerous people call in one week asking me to come into their regions and states to speak at different churches and conferences. The neat thing was that every single person asked me to come in and do something completely different. One group asked me to preach revival and another asked if I would come and prophesy over their people. Someone asked me to do a four-day healing crusade while another wanted me to come and preach for a few days on prayer, etc. Through that time, the Lord showed me that He wanted to train me to walk in all of His fullness. He wants that in every place I go, I would manifest the Kingdom of God and that the presence and glory of the Lord would fill the place.

You see, when the Kingdom-minded believer who walks in God's fullness enters into a place, they are able to impart effectively no matter where or to whom they are sent to minister. At your job, if there are ten people working in different cubicles, you can daily speak life and minister to each one of those people according to their specific needs. All needs are met in the presence of God. My Apostle, Ken Malone, and Apostolic friends like Ryan LeStrange and Jeremy Gibson have preached

numerous times for me in Texarkana, Texas. The ser-
vices are completely different every time each one of
these mighty men of God come to minister! The crowds
are different each time so the needs are different.

I am an Apostle. That is the particular office of
the five-fold ministry in which I walk. It makes perfect
sense to me that the Lord is using people to establish His Kingdom here on earth. Ephesians 2:20 says,
"Having been built on the foundation of the apostles
and prophets, Jesus Christ Himself being the chief cornerstone." Most churches have removed the apostles
and prophets and Jesus Christ as the chief cornerstone.
Numerous ministries and churches have removed the
working of the Holy Spirit. This is why we need reformation and the message of the Kingdom of God—with the
fullness of God—back in the church today. Until we do,
we will lack the power of God to see breakthroughs and
miracles.

Matthew 6:33 says, "But seek first the Kingdom of
God and His righteousness, and all these things shall be
added to you." The word tells us to seek the Kingdom
of God first. Many people do not seek the Kingdom of
God at all. The main problem is that we seek everything
else first when God's word says that when you seek the
Kingdom first, everything else in our lives, ministries,
and businesses will fall into place. In this quest and
study that I am on, I realize that Jesus really had one
central message that He preached: the Kingdom of God.

Luke 4:43 says, "But Jesus said to them, "I must preach the Kingdom of God to the other cities also, because for this purpose I have been sent." The Kingdom of God is mentioned thirty times in the book of Luke. Jesus Christ Himself stated that the main purpose of His coming was to preach and teach the Kingdom of God. Why does the church of today not teach the message Jesus and the apostles taught? Simply because they are disobeying the divine mandate found in Matthew 6:33: "But seek ye first the Kingdom of God, and his righteousness; and all these things shall be added unto you."

This is why the Lord is raising up apostles and prophets again to take up the call to establish the Kingdom of God here on earth. Luke 9:1-2 says, "Then He called His twelve disciples together and gave them power and authority over all demons, and to cure diseases. He sent them to preach the Kingdom of God and to heal the sick." Jesus gave the disciples power and authority over everything that was not of God. Jesus told them to preach the Kingdom of God and to heal every person who was sick. He never told them to pray for the afflicted, because He knew when they taught the Kingdom of God, the presence of the Lord would be manifested bringing healing and deliverance. He knew that the fullness of God would be there and everything would fall into proper alignment the way God intended. Heaven is the place of creation and earth is the place of manifestation!!

Jesus gave very specific instructions to the disciples to preach the Kingdom of God and heal the sick. He knew His purpose was to train and equip these men for the continuation of His ministry here on earth. He empowered them with power and authority from heaven to see the Kingdom of God manifested on earth. Jesus modeled this in Luke 4:43 where it says, "But Jesus said to them, "I must preach the Kingdom of God to the other cities also, because for this purpose I have been sent."

I love the Lord's Prayer especially the first part. Matthew 6:9-10 says, "Our Father in heaven, Hallowed be Your name. Your Kingdom come. Your will be done on earth as it is in heaven." Jesus explains some keys to living a life full of honor and miracles! Jesus identifies God as Father and indicated that He is in Heaven. Then He gives Him honor. Hallowed means "honored as holy, consecrated, to show reverence toward." Then Jesus says, "Your Kingdom come." He is stating that we need the Father's Kingdom to come. We need to place a great priority on asking for the Kingdom of God to be manifested on the earth. Jesus knows what it is like in heaven and now He is on earth. This is why He instructs them to pray as they are taught to in the next verse: "Your will be done on earth as it is in heaven." Because of His love for all mankind, His desire is for God's Kingdom to come and His will to be done here on earth as it is in heaven.

Many people consider the Lord's Prayer to be our model for prayer. If it is indeed the model prayer, it should also be the cry of our heart and anthem by which we live our life. When we have the mindset of the Kingdom of God and understand the supernatural realm that is available to us, we will start to see a phenomenal breakout of miracles everywhere we go. Miracles should actually be a very normal part of our life. Through Christ, we have been empowered to call things back into the right alignment in which God originally created them to be.

We need to learn to declare the word of God over every situation in our lives. As children of God, we should expect for the Kingdom of God to be manifested whenever we decree the promises of the scriptures over any situation and prophesy the word of the Lord over any circumstance. We should expect breakthrough and increase when we speak the word of God by faith.

I really like how Jesus' message of the beatitudes begins and ends with the Kingdom of heaven. Matthew 5:1-3 says, "And seeing the multitudes, He went up on a mountain, and when He was seated, His disciples came to Him. Then He opened His mouth and taught them, saying: "Blessed are the poor in spirit, for theirs is the Kingdom of heaven." The word poor here can also be translated as the word humble which means that those who are humble when they come before the Lord are greatly blessed. These are the people that will do great exploits for God. They know where their gifts, talents, and abilities come from. These people truly understand that the authority and power for all miracles comes from God. Matthew 5:10 says, "Blessed are those who are persecuted for righteousness' sake, for theirs is the Kingdom of heaven." When we stand up for righteousness, the enemy will always try to bring us down. Matthew 6:33 says, "Seek first the Kingdom of God and his righteousness, and everything else will be added unto you." When we seek God's Kingdom, everything else in our lives will fall into place.

Many people try to have everything else fall into place without completely depending on God. God is wanting His people to walk in righteousness, character, and integrity. The men and women of God in these next, upcoming seasons that will walk in the breakthrough power of the Holy Spirit will be people of great humility and authority. This is the way of the Kingdom of God. In a Kingdom there is only one king, ours is named Jesus Christ! All pride, ego, and self must bow to His Lordship and His alone!

The Apostle Paul said in 1 Corinthians 4:20, "For the Kingdom of God is not in word but in power." If you are a citizen of the Kingdom of God, you will have authority and power. Many people are more focused on the things of this earth then the things of heaven. This is why so many do not operate with breakthrough power or in signs, wonders, and miracles. Many people try to force their point of view and opinions upon people in their own natural strength and intelligence, but this is not the way of God's Kingdom. People of His Kingdom think, act, and are very different from those of the Kingdoms of this world.

Jesus Christ preached the message of the Kingdom of God. He did not really preach or teach on anything else. He demonstrated the power of the Kingdom of God more than He talked about it. Jesus did not even really preach healing or deliverance. He just healed people from many different kinds of sicknesses and delivered them from all manner of demonic oppression. This is the message of the Kingdom of God. 1 Corinthians 2:4 says, "And my speech and my preaching were not with persuasive words of human wisdom, but in demonstration of the Spirit and of power." Whenever Jesus walked into a region or place, the entire atmosphere shifted. When we enter a room as children of God, walking in His power and authority and carrying His presence, the whole climate should change for the better. Miracles should start to manifest when true children of God step onto any scene because we are carriers of His presence. Psalm 97:5 tells us that "Mountains melt like wax in the presence of God."

I love the board meeting in Genesis 1, when the Trinity was talking and God said in verse 26, "Let Us make man in Our image, according to Our likeness; let them have dominion." The word dominion in Hebrew is radah which translates into Kingdom. So the Trinity decided to make us in their image and give us Kingdom authority over the earth realm. Many people will never walk in the fullness that God intended them to have because they simply do not understand which Kingdom they are truly from and the authority they have in this world as a result.

I really like what scripture says in Luke 10:19: "Behold, I give you the authority and power to trample on serpents and scorpions, and over all the power of the enemy, and nothing shall by any means hurt you." The first part of this verse is so powerful. Jesus is saying, "I give you authority and power from heaven." My friends, what are you doing with the authority and power from heaven that you have been given? When this verse says that nothing shall be able to come against us and hurt us, do we really believe that? If you did, you would be bold in taking authority over sickness, confusion, oppression, conflicts, and everything around you that does not line up with the word of God. Exercise your God-given authority and walk in the power of the Kingdom of God.

God wants to extend and establish His heavenly Kingdom on earth. He desires to establish His lordship on earth through His sons and daughters. This is why He allowed Adam to name the animals. God wants us to have a daily time to fellowship and communicate with Him. This is why He came down daily to meet with Adam and Eve. The bible says that God came down in the cool of the day to meet with Adam and Eve. He had a standing appointment with them. When they sinned, they immediately began to try to avoid and hide from God, but God was looking for them. God will always look for sons and daughters that are willing to establish the Kingdom of God on earth.

2 Chronicles 16:9 says, "For the eyes of the Lord run to and fro throughout the whole earth, to show Himself strong on behalf of those whose heart is loyal to Him." God is looking to place His favor and blessing upon those who will seek Him with all of their heart for the right reasons. When God finds a loyal heart, He reveals the mysteries of heaven to them and gives them the power to release heaven's atmosphere over entire regions for His greater purpose. We are called to establish the Kingdom of God everywhere we go!

CHAPTER 11
THE FULLNESS OF GOD

I have always had an "I'm all in" kind of personality. I have always wanted to be the best I could possibly be in everything I have ever done. When I really got serious about God at twenty years old, I made up my mind that, if I was going to serve Him, I was going to do so to the fullest. I have had many kairos moments in my walk with the Lord over the past twenty years. I have been a part of life-altering moves of God like the Brownsville Revival and The Ramp and have experienced God in a powerful way every time. I have been blessed to come in contact with very powerful men and women of God over the past twenty-five years. I always looked at these dynamic churches and revival centers as powerful carriers of God's anointing and presence and have told the Lord that I want every bit of it that is available to the fullest measure possible.

One day, I read a scripture that absolutely changed my life. It is found in Ephesians 3:19-20 which says in the Amplified Version, "And [that you may come] to know [practically, through personal experience] the love of Christ which far surpasses [mere] knowledge [without experience], that you may be filled up [throughout your being] to all the fullness of God [so that you may have the richest experience of God's presence in your lives, completely filled and flooded with God Himself]. Now to

Him who is able to [carry out His purpose and] do super-abundantly more than all that we dare ask or think [infinitely beyond our greatest prayers, hopes, or dreams], according to His power that is at work within us."

Verse nineteen is saying that we should know God through personal experience. This revelation grabbed a hold of me and I remember purposing in my heart to lay hold of everything God wanted to give me and allow me to experience. I wanted that experience at the highest degree available. This scripture also says that this experience will be far greater than mere knowledge. When I read this, I remember longing in my heart for the super natural things of God by the Holy Spirit.

When I read the next part of the verse, I could hardly even contain myself. It is a truly amazing thing to realize that we can be completely filled up with the things of God until the point that we are actually overflowing. Then, I remember being brought to laughter and tears all at the same time by the last part of the verse. It was a divine love and joy overload! The last part of this verse tells us that we should be walking in the fullness of God, to the point that we should have the richest experience of God's presence in our lives. God wants us to have and live lives of limitless and measureless power, love, and joy that can only be found in Christ Jesus. Finally, this verse tells us that we should be completely, one hundred percent filled and flooded with God Himself.

Now, if verse nineteen did not put you into a personal revival full of miracles, then verse twenty will for sure! It promises that God will do superabundantly more than we could ever dare to ask or think. I have seen God work in my life to the point where He has done superabundantly far greater than I could have ever even imagined. This comes as no surprise to those who have a close walk with God because it is exactly what He promised to do for every believer who keeps their heart (spirit, mind, and emotions) focused steadfastly on Him. The word think in verse twenty actually got me thinking because I have a huge imagination and am a prophetic dreamer. If you partner with God and allow Him to dream through you, all your dreams will come to pass and with the greatest of measure. In the next part of this verse, the Lord promises to surpass all of our greatest prayers, hopes, and dreams according to His mighty power at work within us. My friends, I have just shared with you one of the greatest breakthrough and miracle scriptures in the bible. If you are not seeing miracles and breakthrough, it is because you are not dreaming, hoping, praying, thinking, and asking for them. If you will do these things, you will find that they are readily available to us in Christ Jesus. Our God has never lied, nor will He ever lie. Get your faith up and allow God to do superabundantly above and beyond everything you could ever imagine.

As children of God, we must learn to think with a Kingdom mindset. So many times we get a prophetic destiny or dream from God and then try to carry it out in the natural realm with natural solutions, but it never works. We have to learn to keep our focus on the Kingdom of God. When something comes from God, it can only be sustained by Him. Matthew 6:22 says, "The lamp of the body is the eye: if therefore thine eye be single, thy whole body shall be full of light." As long as we keep our gaze upon the Lord, we will never get off track. The eye is the lamp of the body. If your eyes are healthy, your whole body will be full of light. What happens is that sometimes we receive a prophetic word from God in the supernatural realm, then try to carry it out with our natural mind in the earthly realm. However, the problem we run into is that the things from the Lord that were given to us by His Spirit cannot be processed by our natural understanding.

James 1:8 says, "A double minded man is unstable in all his ways." You cannot have your mind on the Kingdom of God and the things of this world at the same time. When faced with situations that cannot be handled with our natural strength and understanding, we need to make up our mind that we will call upon the Lord, because that is where our help comes from as Psalm 121:1 tells us. So many times, people are double-minded because they are trying to figure things out naturally when they should be praying about it spiritually. I have often seen people who were so excited at first about what God had spoken and promised to them. They believed God with all their heart. They started moving toward the things of God more and more because they believed the report of the Lord. But a few weeks or months later, they were completely off track.

If you went to the eye doctor and were told you had double vision, it would be a very bad thing. A healthy eye has single vision. Some live out-of-focus in their lives because their eyes are seeing with double vision. If you try to focus on God's Kingdom as well as your own, you will have double vision. Many people need to receive a breakthrough in their mind and be healed from being pulled in more than one direction at the same time. You cannot live a successful Christian life being double-minded. You cannot effectively press toward the prize of the mark of the upward call of God in Christ Jesus if you are striving after more than one ultimate goal and vision for your life at the same time. You have to make a firm decision to submit every other goal and vision to God's divine plan and will for your life. Ask God for grace to know clearly what it is and to serve Him with single-ness of mind and heart. You have to serve God with your all and trust Him with everything you are and have. You need to fully depend on Him to make a way for you in every area of your life. If you are focused on the Kingdom of God, you will remain stable in every area—mentally, emotionally, spiritually, physically, etc.—and live an extremely focused and effective life!

Take a moment to stop and ask yourself the following two questions: what is at the very center of your life and what are you focusing on? Many times, we do not get our breakthrough because our mind is held captive by so many opinions and thoughts that are not from God. If you focus on the Kingdom of God and not this earthly Kingdom, you will experience a greater measure of freedom in your life from distractions and double-mindedness than you have ever had before.

Matthew 6:33 says, "Seek first the Kingdom of God and His righteousness, and all other things shall be added unto you." When you focus your life on the Kingdom vision that God has given you, you can expect to have provision in every area made available to you all the days of your life. Remember that God has called you for such a time as this to stand up for Him and let your life be counted upon. Focus on the Kingdom purpose for which you were created. Our world is in need of people walking in the authority and power of God. Stay focused on your Kingdom function and remain single-minded after God and the things of His Kingdom!

If a person is married, but starts looking at someone that is not their spouse, it means they are going back on their vow and are being double-minded. It means their focus is divided between two people. When this happens it brings division. When you are married, you are supposed to be committed one hundred and ten percent! When you are not fully committed, your sight starts to get blurry and you begin to lose focus. It can be the same way with a job. When you are not satisfied, you will start actively looking for another job on your days off. Oftentimes, your production will even begin to decline on your current job. But not so when it comes to your divine Kingdom spouse and assignment, in Jesus' mighty name! This is a time in which you will need to focus in on God's heart for you in this season. If you focus on the things of the flesh more than on the things of the Holy Spirit, you will lose focus. Determine from today that with God's help and strength, you will remain steadfastly fixed on the things of His Kingdom and righteousness. Not only will you be kept in the center of God's will for your life, but God Himself will see to it that every other thing you will ever be in need of will be added unto you!

CHAPTER 12
GOD CONFIDENCE

Romans 15:29 says, "And I am sure that, when I come unto you, I shall come in the fullness of the blessing of the Jesus Christ." I really admire the confidence Apostle Paul had in God. Here is a man who did not walk in his own strength or wisdom, but fully and completely relied on the power of the Lord. Paul was so confident in God that he told the people in advance that when he reached them, he would be walking and moving in the spirit of God in presenting the gospel of Jesus Christ. Paul's example shows us that one person can truly walk in the fullness of God and be completely filled with the gifts and fruit of the Spirit.

I love the book of Acts because of the raw demonstration of the power of God readily available to us as followers and sent ones of Jesus Christ. Many powerful men and women of God I know, ask the spiritual leadership wherever they go to minister to have the people fast and pray so that they will come in the power and authority of God in signs, wonders and miracles. This is not confidence in ourselves nor in our gifting but, rather, it demonstrates boldness and great faith in the raw power of God. We need people in every walk of life that are full of faith to believe that God can—and will—do everything He said He would do. This world needs people who will boldly declare God's word with great confidence in His power to fulfill it.

Paul already told this group of people that when he came to their town to minister to them, he planned to impart spiritual gifts to them that would bear lasting fruit in their lives. Romans 1:11 says, "For I long to see you, that I may impart unto you some spiritual gifts, to the end that you will be established." I love the fact that the Apostle Paul never relied on his own strength, but leaned on God at all times. He was a man who lived a life of prayer and fasting. When we know who we are in Christ, we will start to walk in a God-confidence and will see great breakthroughs in our atmospheres and awesome miracles in our midst. These will start to happen on a regular basis and become a normal part of our everyday lives.

Get ready! Kingdom increase is coming to many with great Kingdom breakthroughs for God's Kingdom purposes!

JOE JOE DAWSON MINISTRIES

JOEJOEDAWSON.NET

Facebook
JOEJOEDAWSONTXK

Instagram
@JOE_JOE_DAWSONTXK

Periscope
@JOEJOEDAWSON

YouTube
JOE JOE DAWSON

Roar Apostolic Network is a network of believers who are contending for revival and awakening. Our heart is to help train and equip every person and ministry that comes into alignment with us. We are called to walk in the fullness of God's authority and power while abiding in the Father's love. Our calling is to help others reach their God-given dreams and destiny. This network is built for any church, ministry, pastor, business person, intercessor, believer, etc. ROAR stands for Revival, Outpouring, Awakening, and Reformation.
For more information, visit roarapostolicnetwork.com

Roar Church is an Apostolic community of believers passionate about the Kingdom of God in Texarkana, Texas. It was founded in 2017 by Apostle Joe Joe & Autumn Dawson. Roar Church is a gathering of believers seeking the presence and power of God together. It is our desire for revival, outpouring, awakening and reformation to transform our region and see the Kingdom of God manifested in the earth. For more information , visit roarchurchtexarkana.com

All of Joe Joe Dawson's books have been administrated by
McFarland Creative. McFarland Creative offers full book
facilitation that includes book editing, interior design,
formatting & cover design. We will take your vision for the
book inside of you and make it a reality. If you are
interested in sharing your words with the world,
email info@mcfarland-creative.com today!